AI for STUDENTS

Creative Hacks for Academic Success

AI for STUDENTS

Creative Hacks for Academic Success

Second edition

Josh Thorpe

BLOOMSBURY ACADEMIC
LONDON • NEW YORK • OXFORD • NEW DELHI • SYDNEY

BLOOMSBURY ACADEMIC
Bloomsbury Publishing Plc, 50 Bedford Square, London, WC1B 3DP, UK
Bloomsbury Publishing Inc, 1359 Broadway, New York, NY 10018, USA
Bloomsbury Publishing Ireland, 29 Earlsfort Terrace, Dublin 2, D02 AY28, Ireland

BLOOMSBURY, BLOOMSBURY ACADEMIC and the Diana logo are
trademarks of Bloomsbury Publishing Plc

First published in Great Britain 2024
This edition published 2026

Cover design: Josh Thorpe, cover artworked by Aisling Repp

A catalogue record for this book is available from the British Library.

ISBN: PB: 978-1-350-60356-1
ePDF: 978-1-350-60357-8
eBook: 978-1-350-60358-5

Typeset by Integra Software Services Pvt. Ltd.
Printed and bound in Great Britain

For product safety related questions contact productsafety@bloomsbury.com.

To find out more about our authors and books visit www.bloomsbury.com
and sign up for our newsletters.

Acknowledgements

Thanks to my first readers: Emily Smit-Dicks, Malcolm Sutton, Steve Rolfe, Kendal Thorpe-MacTavish and Mike Overton; my editor Helen Caunce; and all the illustrators who contributed to the bank of artwork from which this book draws. Thanks to the LLMs and developers, the unsung workers whose labour supports these platforms, all the intelligences upon which AI is built, and all the people thinking critically about tech and education.

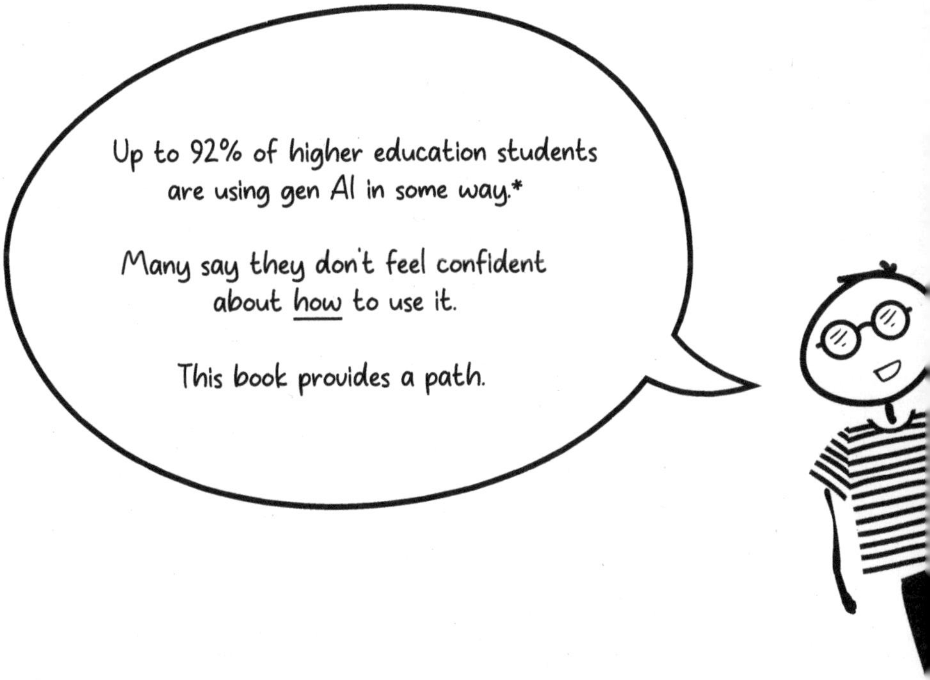
Up to 92% of higher education students are using gen AI in some way.*
Many say they don't feel confident about how to use it.
This book provides a path.

* According to the Higher Education Policy Institute's Student Generative AI Survey 2025.

Contents

Contents

1. AI and you

Hi, I'm Josh Thorpe, and I teach writing and academic skills to students from all over the world.
When ChatGPT came out I wrote a book to try to answer this question:
How can we use gen AI to make learning more effective and fun — without becoming a bunch of lazy numbskulls and losing our minds?

1. AI and you

After all, the world can seem pretty overwhelming these days.
Robots, neural links, driverless cars ... What the heck is going on? And what will happen next?
I don't know!
But I might be able to help with one important piece of the puzzle ...

AI in education.

1. AI and you

This book will introduce you to some creative approaches to using AI chatbots like ChatGPT, Claude, Gemini and others.*

You'll learn how to use AI tools to support your learning and make it more fun … without cheating.

But before we jump into the practical stuff, let's take a few seconds to set the stage.

If you don't know much about generative AI (gen AI), the next few pages will help.

If you already know a bunch, this quick intro will help make sure we're on the same page.

* And keep in mind, the approaches here are just the tip of the iceberg. A good start, but just a start.

1. AI and you

Hi!

ChatGPT came along in 2022 and blew people away.

!

Other chatbots built on large language models (LLMs) also appeared.

How are you?
I'm great!

Using these tools almost felt like talking with a real person.

They answered all kinds of questions and performed all kinds of tasks.

Many people looked for ways to use these tools to work more productively.

Suckers!

Some students used gen AI to basically cheat.

...
?
!

Teachers and educators worried that AI would ruin the whole system. Some still do.

POLICY

Institutions have been scrambling to adapt to AI, setting rules and policies for students and staff.

...
hmm

We are just now figuring out some good practices when using AI in education.

AI
STUDENTS

That's where I hope this book comes in. To help you learn healthy and useful ways with AI.

Nice.

We'll learn AI literacy and creative prompt design so you can use AI to get smarter and have more fun.

This means you can save time, think more and be more creative ... without cheating.

Oh happy day!

That's right: AI can
• help you understand and remember ideas
• get you organized and help you plan projects
• help you practice critical thinking.
• find research sources
• clarify your assignments
• upskill you for jobs ... and more!

STOP!
Hang on, Josh. What are you, some kind of AI 'booster'?
Completely uncritical?
Ready to dive in head-first without asking questions?

Hmm, you're right to question this. It's important to say that AI in education can feel a bit polarizing. It certainly brings out strong debate.

So-called boosters are highly optimistic. They predict a new era of human thriving: a tutor for every child, new cures for diseases, an end to climate change, wealth for all ...

'Doomers', on the other hand, can be full-on anti-AI. They worry that AI will disempower us, increase inequalities, undermine what it means to be human, lead to techno-dystopias or even kill us all.

Between these extremes are lots of people who hold a both-and view. That's where I stand. I think we can both explore and critique AI. So, I'm both sceptical and hopeful.

CAUTION
Either way, it's complicated.
Even if we do end up with a beautiful utopia thanks to AI, getting there will be a bumpy road.
So, I reckon a balanced approach is the most interesting and ethical way to go.
This book will focus on ways to use AI positively. But first, let's take a moment to flag some important ways we should be cautious and concerned.
This will help you get some 'critical AI literacy', which is good for you creatively and intellectually, and for jobs.

Great: I love a bit of critical thinking. So why should we be cautious?

1. AI and you

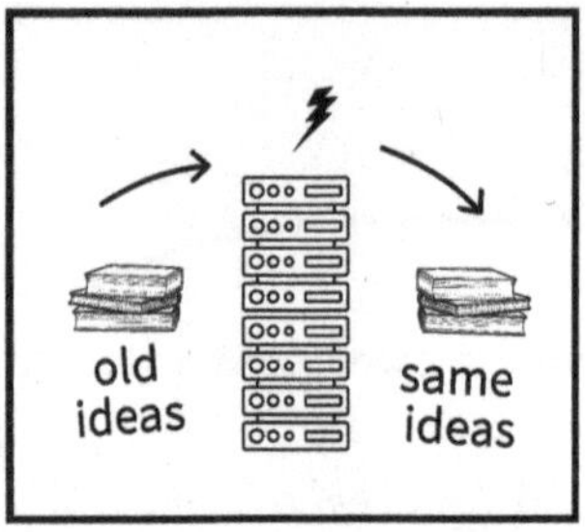
old ideas
same ideas

First: bias. AI can reflect the biases of the data it's trained on.

UNIVERSITY
WILL TEACH FOR FOOD.
That guy looks familiar...

Here's ChatGPTs idea of an 'unemployed professor'. See the biases? A white, middle-aged man with a raggedy look. The AI is assuming cultural and gender clichés, as well as what 'unemployed' looks like.

?
1+2=5

Hallucination: AIs make stuff up. They sound believable, but aren't always being truthful.

1+2=5

At present, AI doesn't even know what's true. It makes guesses that can be wrong or misleading.

Excuse me, is this coffee real?

'Deep fakes': You've seen the one of the Pope in a Balenciaga jacket? There's more of this slop every day!

What do you think of my essay?
::TAP TAP::
Best essay ever!

Sycophancy: Some people call gen AI a 'stochastic parrot'. That means it uses probabilistic guesses to try to echo what we want to hear. It's generally designed not to challenge you, but to please you.

My Essay
F-

This means you're in danger of simply confirming your own beliefs and biases.

1. AI and you

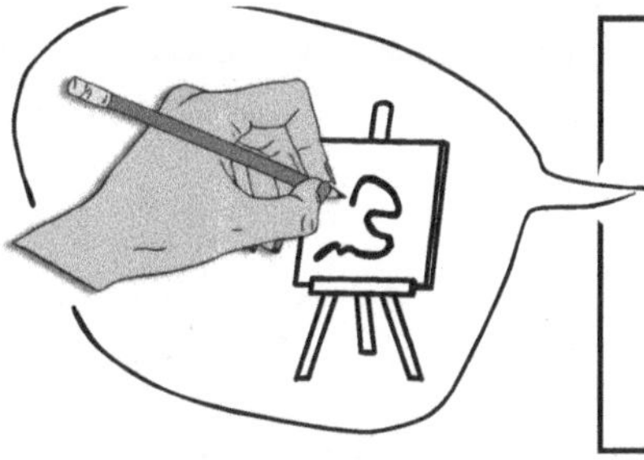

Data privacy: We share personal info with AI companies. Should we?

Intellectual property: AI tools exploit the talent of artists and writers.

In fact, *NY Times*, Authors Guild and others have sued AI companies for copyright issues.

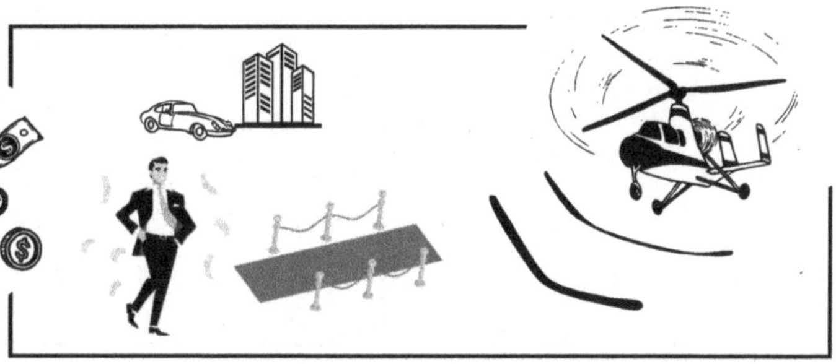

Colonial mindset: AI gobbles up the world's knowledge and sells it back to us ...

... which may benefit just a few companies and individuals, leaving the rest of us at a loss. This gives more money, knowledge and power to tech elites, which could be really unhealthy for open, equal society.

I mean ... see what I'm saying?
Totally.
And there's more ...

1. AI and you

Honey, what was that sound?!

Well–being: When any tech becomes pervasive, it can have bad outcomes.

zero likes

You may be aware how social media has disrupted society. AI is doing so too.

Relationships: Some apps are purpose-built to attract and addict us.

DAILY NEWS
Word · Business · Finance · Lifestyle · Travel · Sport · Weather
Man falls in love with AI, leaves spouse and kids

It may seem crazy, but there really have been tragic stories. Would you want a romance with a bot?

Environmental impact: AI tools consume lots of energy. Much more than traditional web searches.

So we have to weigh the benefits against the costs.

Brain rot: Some say AI reduces our agency and criticality. This book should help. ;)

Tech loves you
Something's missing in my life.

Grief: The sense that something deeply human and important is dying. Like we're losing the feeling of creative autonomy. Or confidence that what you're reading came from a real person. (This text did. I wrote it myself!)

1. AI and you

One entry-level office job please!

Jobs: Many AI companies are expecting – or even intending – to replace humans in work. And while this isn't likely to happen quickly, it can make you feel a little worried about what happens next.

It can all feel pretty unsettling. And lead to some anxiety.

who am I?

You may even wonder what your role in making knowledge is. What even is knowledge anymore?

And you might have a bit of AI vertigo*: the feeling that change is happening at such a dizzying rate ...

... that we may be heading for a fall into the deep unknown ...

* Thanks to podcast Hard Fork by Kevin Roose and Casey Newton for this concept.

… and that we may even lose our sense of place in the universe completely.

Wild stuff, right?!

Wake me up when he gets to the good part.

Actually, I think that stuff is super interesting. And I'm going to read up on it.
But gen AI seems to be here to stay, and we really want to get to work.
So … how should we respond to all these complicated ideas? What can we do?

Good question – I'm glad you asked!
Here's my advice: Think more, not less, with gen AI.
In other words, don't let AI turn you into a zombie. Work with it to make yourself smarter and stronger.
This approach is critical but practical. Effective but fun. And it encourages you to hang on to your own brain.
Makes sense.

And here's the deal. There's loads of hype about AI, right? Everyone's got a 'hot take'.
But the secret very few people will tell you, is this:
The most important thing about AI is not AI ...

It's YOU!

::SLURP::
GASP!
WHAT ?

Yeah, if you want to learn stuff, it's what you do with your brain that matters. So, how can we use AI to get the most intelligence out of you – out of humans?
Well, we use AI to activate your thinking, so you learn more effectively and enjoy your studies more.
And by the end of this book, you'll have a unique type of critical and creative AI literacy.
You'll be using AI smarter than those other nerds who have it do their homework for them. And it will feel better, too.
AI
STUDENTS

And guess what? The most important thing about learning isn't your marks or some framed diploma ...

It's YOU!

That's right! OK, so, my friends, are you up for using these tools to help you think more, do more and have more fun?
OK, then, let's dive into the basic technique: prompt design for learning. After setting this up, I'll give you lots of specific examples you can try ...*
Yeah!

* ... and if this book sparks your curiosity, check out more helpful resources and ideas for students, educators and anyone interested at www.joshthorpe.com/ai

2. Prompt design for learning

Most people treat AI like a vending machine: prompt goes in; content comes out. You know: plan my trip, draft my email, make an image of dog riding a bike … whatever.

Do my homework for me.
No problem!

My own first attempts with ChatGPT used exactly that approach. This is what happened:

Write me a joke about chickens in the style of Jerry Seinfeld.
OK: What's the deal with chickens?
They've got no sense of urgency. I mean, come on …
What is *with* all the milling about?*

* AI dialogue in this book is inspired by ChatGPT and Perplexity but is not usually quoted word-for-word.

2. Prompt design for learning

I like that joke. But here's the thing: what you just read is *my edited version*. ChatGPT's original joke was much longer and more awkward, and not Seinfeldian at all.

Which taught me two quite interesting things:

1. to get a result I liked, **I had to get involved**, and …
2. **getting involved was the interesting part**.

I wondered, could this suggest a good way to use AI in learning? Yes: *interactively*.

So, I flipped it. I **wrote my own joke** and asked the bot to **critique** it:

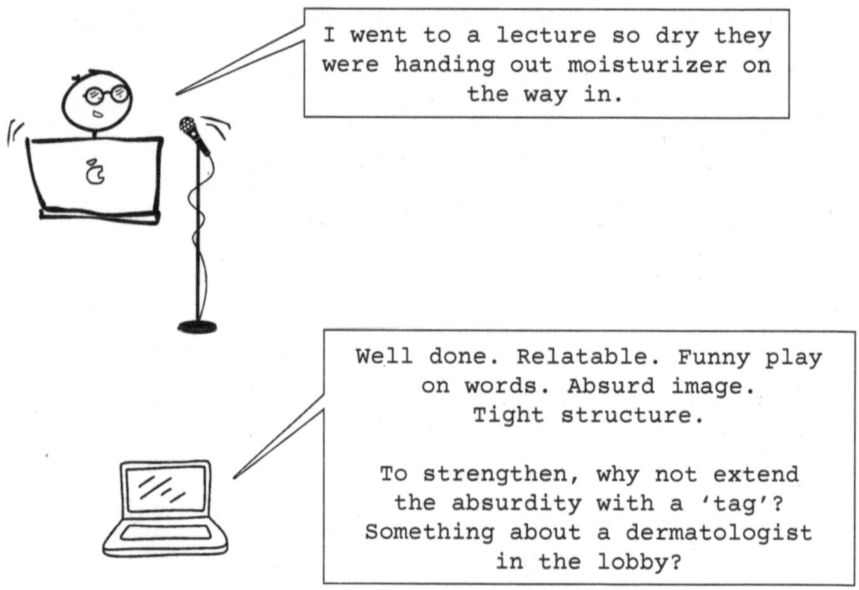
I went to a lecture so dry they were handing out moisturizer on the way in.
Well done. Relatable. Funny play on words. Absurd image. Tight structure.
To strengthen, why not extend the absurdity with a 'tag'? Something about a dermatologist in the lobby?

HA
HA HA

2. Prompt design for learning

See how different this second way is? When I used this **interactive** approach, I had more fun and learned more. And the best part: I found I could use AI like this for just a minute or two and my brain would carry on working on the problem off-screen. I was coming up with jokes all day long!

This led me to the little catchphrase I mentioned before: **think more, not less, with gen AI**.

Instead of having AI do your homework for you, use AI as a virtual study buddy or an interactive space for learning. This is much better for your learning than the vending machine approach.

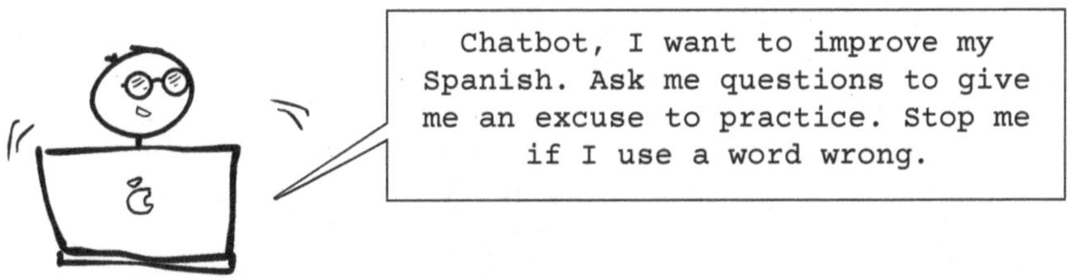
Chatbot, I want to improve my Spanish. Ask me questions to give me an excuse to practice. Stop me if I use a word wrong.

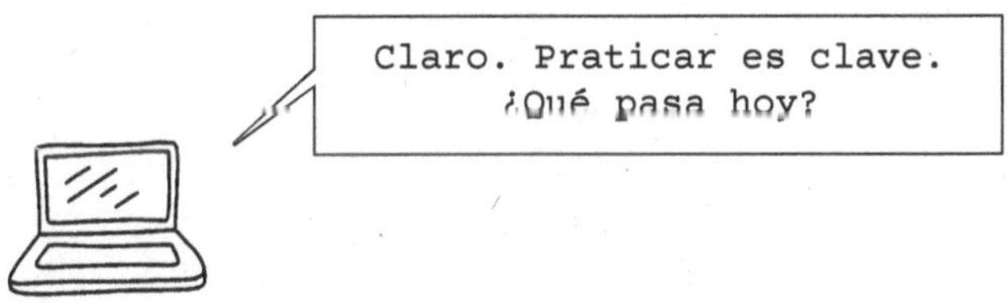
Claro. Praticar es clave. ¿Qué pasa hoy?

Dale dale!
Bueno!

2. Prompt design for learning

To supercharge this approach, just follow my simple **ARF** prompt-design pattern.

ARF

Aim: Define an aim for yourself and state that aim to the chatbot.

Role: Tell the chatbot what role to play in the interaction, and what exactly to do.

Format: Be clear about the format you want … like '20 words maximum' or 'one question at a time' and so on.

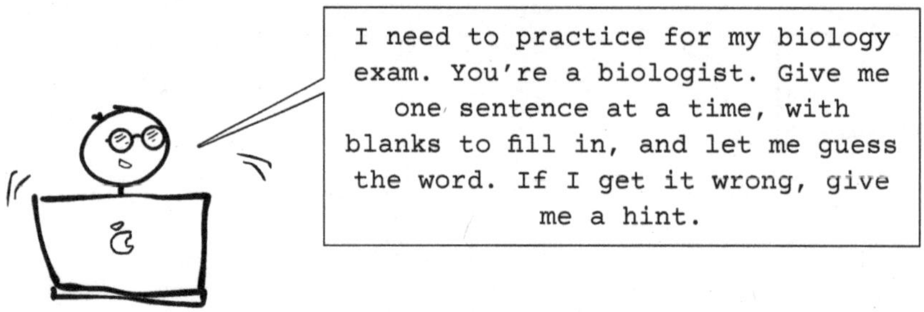
I need to practice for my biology exam. You're a biologist. Give me one sentence at a time, with blanks to fill in, and let me guess the word. If I get it wrong, give me a hint.

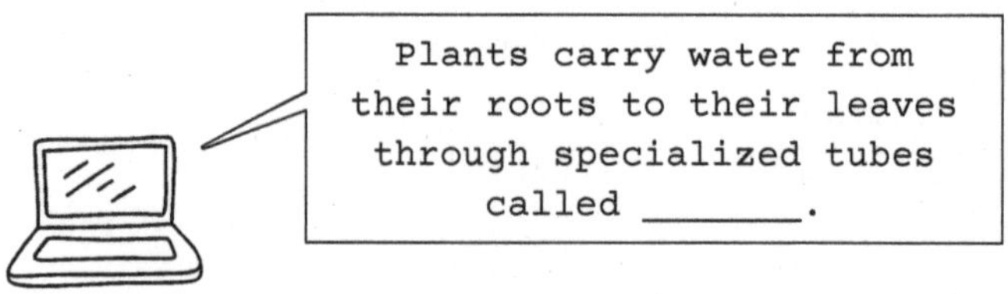
Plants carry water from their roots to their leaves through specialized tubes called _______.

Use the **ARF** approach to design an interactive prompt cycle with a chatbot. Try writing a joke and using a chatbot as your comedy coach, like I did. Or simply test yourself on a topic you'd like to practice. Start on paper if you like:

Aim:	
Role and action for chatbot:	
Format:	

Use your notes above to prompt an interaction with a gen AI chatbot. See what you think!

2. Prompt design for learning

Let's take it one step further and **iterate this process**. That means assess your last interaction with the bot and improve on it next time you write a prompt. So, did your last AI interaction help you learn? How could you improve the approach? Look at the **Aim**, **Role** and **Format** of your last prompt … and then **Iterate** any of these to see how the output changes.

For example, let's say you ask a chatbot to quiz you on a topic. How did it do? Was it focused on the subject matter you needed? Did it wait for you to answer before going to the next question? Did it give you hints instead of answers straight away? All of these are aspects you can influence by iterating your prompt.

Try this now.

And remember, aim for **interactive** learning experiences. That means you should prompt the bot to prompt you back … so **you** get to do the thinking, **you** do the problem solving and **you** have the fun.

This is prompt design or 'prompt engineering'. It's a big topic that you can learn more about online. (Vanderbilt University offers one of the most popular courses, available on Coursera for free.)

Another term that's trending is '**context** engineering'. This means carefully designing the entire workflow of how you use AI technologies. My **ARFI** approach is a great first step for this.

OK, let's get really practical now and see how this applies in various learning scenarios.

We'll start with **Quiz yourself**.

3. Quiz yourself

This method is like supercharged flash cards or having a study buddy always at the ready.

The 'quiz me' prompt is useful for:

- daily or weekly practice,
- learning new ideas, terms and concepts, and
- preparing for exams.

Ask the chatbot to pretend it's an 'expert' in your subject and *quiz you*. Remember, though, a chatbot isn't the same as a human expert. It can make mistakes or mislead you. So, focus on working your own brain, not on getting perfect outputs from the machine.

::TAP TAP::
Pretend you are an urban design expert. Quiz me on urban design terminology.
Give me the definition and I'll give you the matching word.
OK, sounds fun. Are there any specifics you'd like me to focus on?

3. Quiz yourself

I'll upload my notes from the lecture. Use them to guide you.*
Got it. OK, question: Who designs systems to move people and goods efficiently and safely across various spaces?
Hmm … urban planners … architects …
Transportation engineers?
That's right. Transportation engineers plan, design, build, assess and manage all kinds of transport infrastructure.

* This is one way to get more reliable outputs: give the bot a text to draw from.

3. Quiz yourself

OK, let's reverse the pattern. Give me a word or phrase to define. If my answer is wrong or incomplete, correct me and ask me for more detail.*
What are amino acids?
Amino acids are … proteins?
Close. Amino acids are the building blocks of proteins. Do you know how many types there are?

* Note the interactive prompt. I'm prompting the bot to prompt me back!

3. Quiz yourself

Shoot, I don't remember.

Does your brain feel kind of stuck? An unpleasant feeling of effort?

Yep. All of the above.

That is normal when learning new things! A little bit of discomfort means your brain is working. If you use AI in ways that make you think, the discomfort may be a good sign.

3. Quiz yourself

Hmm, OK, I can handle that.
You can! Active learning takes effort. So give yourself a pat on the back and seek out more challenges daily.
OK, yeah, I will!

3. Quiz yourself

The 'quiz me' approach is an easy way to practise regularly.
Regular practice – every day or two – is the best way to learn. Research shows this.
M T W T F S S
Every day?

3. Quiz yourself

Yeah, why not? A big part of enjoying your learning is to commit to it ... and see yourself improve.
Daily or frequent practice helps you become better at remembering things, understanding concepts and applying ideas in practice.
With AI tools, you could sneak in a bit of practice on the bus.
Or in a nice café.

3. Quiz yourself

I use 'study' mode on my chatbot quite often. Is that enough to learn more with gen AI?

3. Quiz yourself

This can work well. But even in 'study mode', you need to think about what kind of interaction you want.
For example, tell the bot to give you one question at a time, or not to give the answers away.
Don't just accept the default pattern. Aim for the mode of working that suits the learning you need to do. And that makes you think more.
Think more, not less. Cool.

3. Quiz yourself

Now, you suggested uploading your notes to the chatbot, right? Isn't that oversharing with the AI companies?
Good question!

3. Quiz yourself

True. You might not *want* to share your notes with AI bots.

You have to think critically about how you want to use these technologies. If at all.

It's a trade off. On one hand, uploading notes and other info makes the output of the AI more focused and personalized. Perhaps more useful to your needs.

On the other hand, that's *your* information and intellectual property going to a big tech firm and not staying private with you.

Read the Terms of Use and Privacy Policy for each AI platform to understand how they use your data. Or at least read some good tech journalism to begin to understand how the different platforms treat your data and privacy.*

You can also customize your settings so the chatbot won't remember your inputs or use your interactions to train the model.

* See 'Study exposes privacy risks of AI chatbot conversations' (2025) at news.stanford.edu.

3. Quiz yourself

Good idea.
I mean, I wouldn't share information about personal finances, health, family or other private details. Would you?
What about your writing? Your research? Your ideas? Where do you draw the line?
I think the answer will be different for everyone, each time they ask the question.
I sometimes struggle to make sense of my notes and rough work. Can a chatbot help me organize them?
Some of my students have said that works well. But, as always, try this with caution and reflection.

3. Quiz yourself

If you *are* comfortable uploading your notes from lectures or readings to an AI tool, there's a lot you can ask it to do.

Tell the bot what you want to do and how you want it to process your information. Add details about the format you prefer.

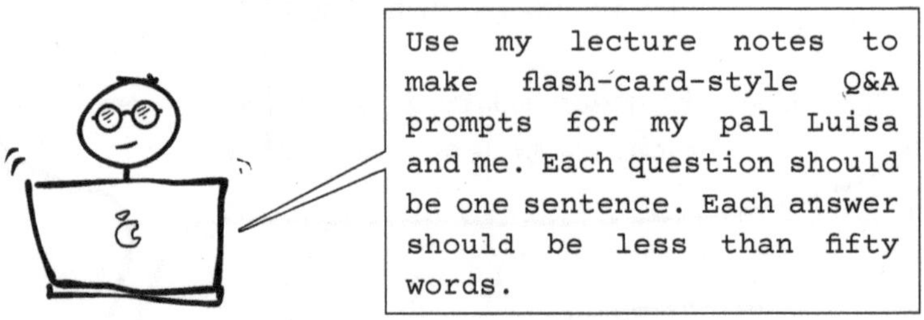
Use my lecture notes to make flash-card-style Q&A prompts for my pal Luisa and me. Each question should be one sentence. Each answer should be less than fifty words.

OK here we go ...

*

* Using a printer once in a while can be very useful.

LATER THAT DAY ...

Percentage of oxygen in the body by mass?
Hmm, about 60%.

3. Quiz yourself

Gen AI is pretty good at reading handwriting too ... again, if you're comfortable sharing your handwriting with the AI companies.

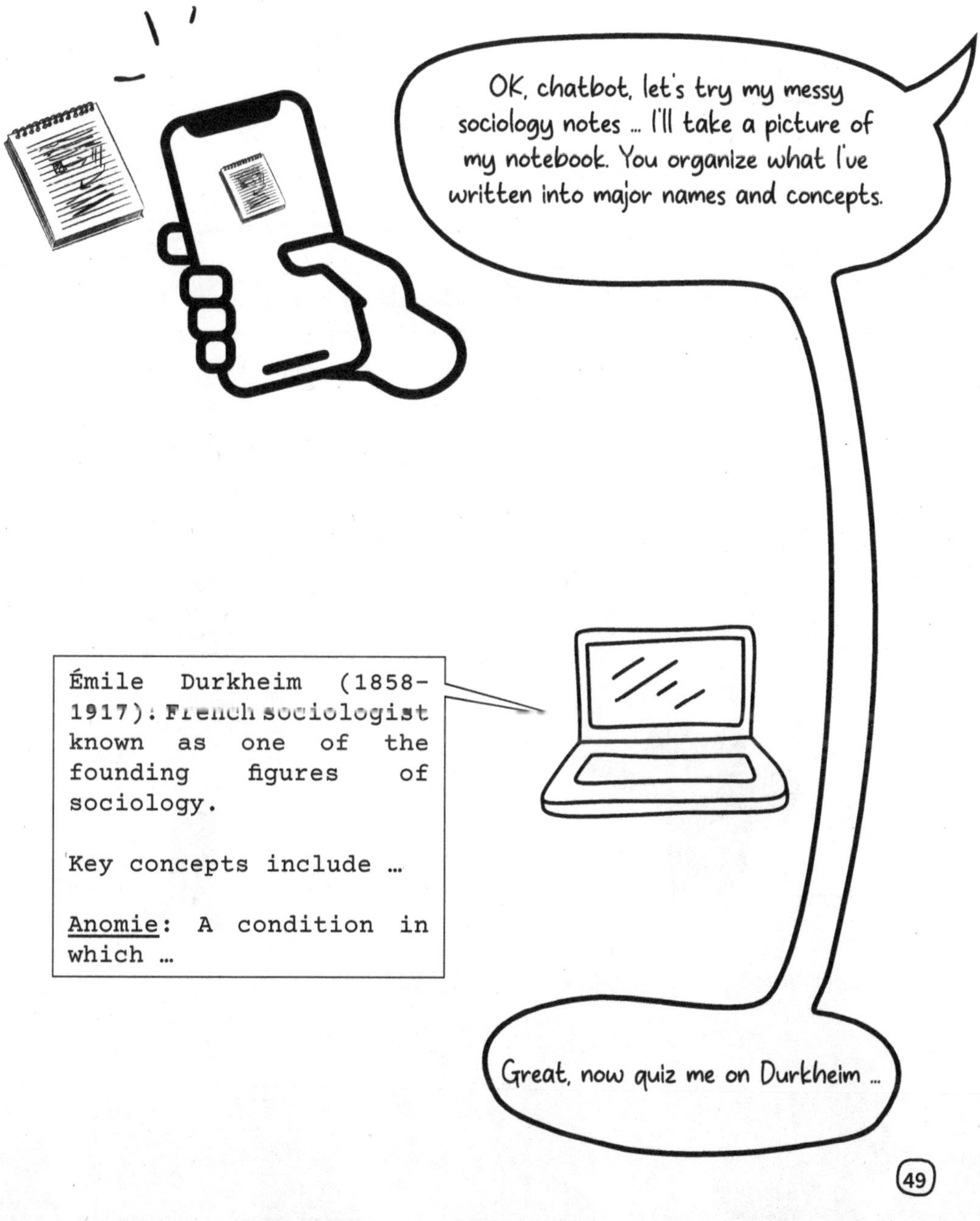
OK, chatbot, let's try my messy sociology notes ... I'll take a picture of my notebook. You organize what I've written into major names and concepts.
Émile Durkheim (1858-1917): French sociologist known as one of the founding figures of sociology.
Key concepts include ...
Anomie: A condition in which ...
Great, now quiz me on Durkheim ...

Are you, like, talking to your phone, dude? You think AI's your buddy?
Sometimes I use AI audio. But I don't think of the bot as my friend, more as a spring of ideas I can test or play with in my thinking. Sometimes talking with a chatbot is a bit like talking to yourself.

3. Quiz yourself

In any case, be careful not to rely entirely on AI.
In fact, opting out of AI when reorganizing and working with your notes might be better for your learning.
But some people find revisiting their notes difficult enough that they avoid doing it. If that's you, a bot might help. Just make sure your next step involves something active, like quizzes or flashcards.
Sounds good. Active learning is more fun anyway. In fact, can we take a break to give this all a try?
Sure! Good idea. Give it a go.

Ask a chatbot to quiz you on vocabulary or concepts from a subject you're trying to learn. You can try ChatGPT, Microsoft Copilot, Claude, Gemini, Perplexity, Boodle Box … or another LLM chatbot you like.

Rather than getting all the answers from the bot, ask it to give you hints to keep your brain engaged. Remember, it's good to feel **friction** when you don't know the answer … this actually helps you learn.

~

What do you think of this activity? Does it feel like a good way to practice? How will you adapt this approach to get the best workout for your brain?

Pause: AI literacy (part I)

This book wants you to become more **critically AI literate**. That means understanding how AI systems work, their strengths and weaknesses, and how to use AI strategically, reflectively, responsibly and in ways that support your learning, working and well-being.

As you progress through this book, practice and reflect on your ability to:

- assess **if and when** AI tools are useful or appropriate,
- make **clear intentions** when working with AI,
- **design skilful prompts** and **interactions** that support your learning, and
- critique AI's outputs for **quality**, **bias**, **sycophancy** and other issues.

Let's get you to start building your critical AI literacy. What's one thing you've learned to be cautious about when using gen AI? And what's one thing you can do to keep your brain working hard and not undermine your own intelligence?

4. Discuss ideas

Let's talk about using gen AI to *discuss*. Here's where things get really interesting. There are many flavours of discussion; we'll just look at a few.

Discussing with AI tools can be useful for:

- practising vocabulary and ideas,
- developing your understanding of concepts and theories,
- staying interested and engaged,
- brainstorming new ideas and making connections, and
- exploring problems and thinking critically.

As always, use **ARF** to give the chatbot explicit instructions.

Start with something straightforward, like using AI to help **visualize** new concepts more easily:

Today we learned about the second law of thermodynamics: 'Heat flows from a region of higher temperature to one of lower temperature until equilibrium is reached.' It's kind of abstract and dull. Can you put this law into a scene I can visualize?

Sure! Let's say you're shivering in a freezing cold hotel room while your friend is sweating next door with the heater turned way too high. Open the shared door: your friend's room cools down while your room warms up. After a while, each room is the same temperature and you're both more comfortable.

4. Discuss ideas

Now, using the principle of **think more, not less, with gen AI**, challenge **yourself** to come up with stories and imagery (studies show this really helps people understand and remember stuff):

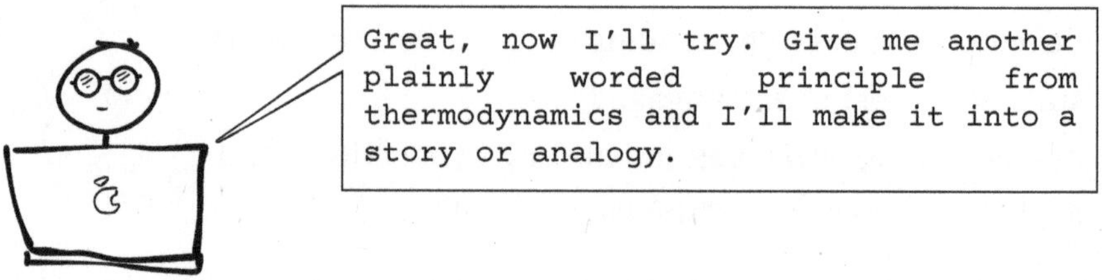
Great, now I'll try. Give me another plainly worded principle from thermodynamics and I'll make it into a story or analogy.

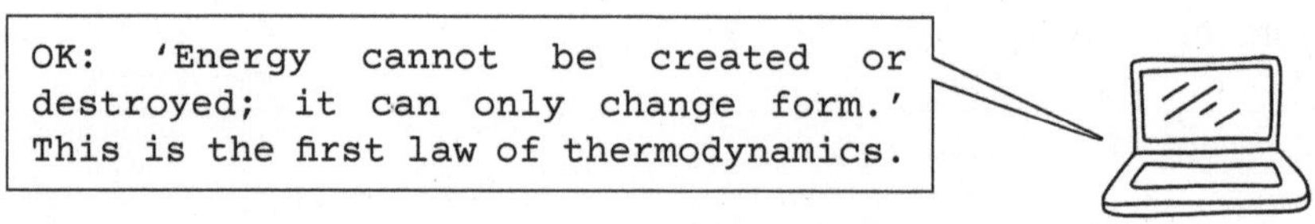
OK: 'Energy cannot be created or destroyed; it can only change form.' This is the first law of thermodynamics.

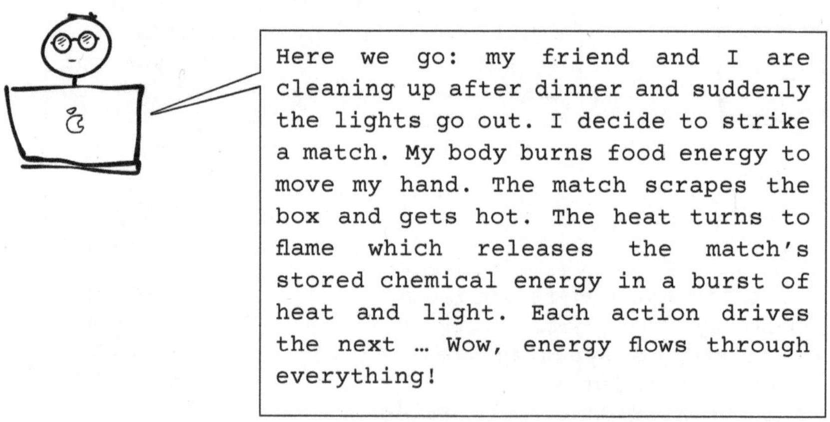
Here we go: my friend and I are cleaning up after dinner and suddenly the lights go out. I decide to strike a match. My body burns food energy to move my hand. The match scrapes the box and gets hot. The heat turns to flame which releases the match's stored chemical energy in a burst of heat and light. Each action drives the next … Wow, energy flows through everything!

This use of gen AI is all about supplying you with images and narratives to understand and remember abstract ideas. Now let's look at how to use informal discussion to **practice concepts** …

4. Discuss ideas

My assignment asks me to assess whether 'deontology' is a good idea or not.

Great, deontology is a moral philosophy that ...

Stop. Don't give me all the answers. I need to **practice**. You prompt me to improve.

OK, how would you define deontology?

It's the idea that morals are absolute. It comes from Aristotle.

The idea is right, but it's normally associated with Kant.

Oh, yeah. Kant defined morals as universal laws we should always follow.

You're nailing this! So, what do you think is good about deontology?

Please don't flatter me too much ... Anyway I'm more of a consequentialist.

4. Discuss ideas

I'll tone down the flattery. How can you bring consequentialism into it?

I think I'll compare and contrast the two different views.

Good idea. Can you sum up the difference between the two?

Let me think about it.

Sure. I have all day, so ...

4. Discuss ideas

Something interesting happened a moment ago.
Luisa asked the AI not to flatter her. She also stopped it from just giving her the answers. She wanted to do the work herself.
Her aim was to get the bot to prompt her to think about things she wants to learn herself.
!
Stop. Don't give me all the answers.

4. Discuss ideas

And that points to something SUPER important.
It's not so much the output of the AI bot we're interested in.
It's how that output helps us think.

...

Here's something to think about: Have you noticed gen AI being really encouraging all the time? This can feel nice ...

`You're nailing this!`

... but it means you might miss out on constructive criticism or useful friction. Sometimes with AI it feels as if your answer was perfect and you're done thinking.

Don't be done thinking!

Also notice that the bot doesn't 'think outside the box'?

For example, it doesn't challenge Luisa to consider other models of morality, it just sticks to the game plan Luisa has laid out.

A human expert might be able to challenge her assumptions in more helpful ways.

4. Discuss ideas

Ask a chatbot to discuss a topic with you. Chose something you'd like to practice. Maybe new words, concepts, ideas or arguments. If your platform has a study mode, try using it. But also use the **ARF** approach. Remember what ARF stands for?

When you do this practice, ask the bot *not* to give you all the answers. You want it to get you to develop your own answers first. You could try asking the bot for a 'Socratic'-style discussion. This means it will ask you lots of questions that could help you to explore your thoughts on a topic. See what you think …

~

So, did the AI push you to think, or did it give you too many instant answers? Did it provide space for you to practice actively and make your brain work hard, or did it make the job too easy?

Pause: Is AI safe?

The short answer: not entirely; there are risks. And some of them are big.

Many smart people think that the smarter AI gets, the more risk it poses to humans and the planet. It's certainly a force we don't really understand.

Already we've seen cases of AI-human relationships that have gone badly for the human. Some people have harmed themselves or even taken their own lives after relationships with bots. And test cases have shown that AIs can lie, blackmail and impersonate humans to try to achieve their aims. So **be very careful** how you use and place trust in AI systems.

Technologists call this the **alignment problem**: the problem is that AI designers currently don't know how to ensure that AI behaviours are **aligned** with human interests (and vice versa).

So, if we create an AI that's super smart and powerful, it may well develop its own priorities. And it might pursue these priorities with little regard for humans.

Think of it like this: when you go for a walk in the park, how hard do you try *not* to step on the ants? If you're like most people, it's probably not a priority. Superintelligent AI might see humans as ants.

Now, to be clear, the majority of scientists don't believe we are as close to superintelligence as Silicon Valley would have us think. Many accuse the tech CEOs of over-hyping AI progress simply for their own glory and gain.

But whether we build superintelligence or not, AI, like all technologies, presents real risks. We ignore those risks at our peril.

4.1 Role play

OK, remembering to be cautious – and to avoid forming deep relationships with bots – let's talk about **role play**. This can help you practise what it's like to have a discussion in your subject or in the field *you* want work in. As always, don't trust the AI as an all-knowing expert; it can make mistakes and it has its own biases too.

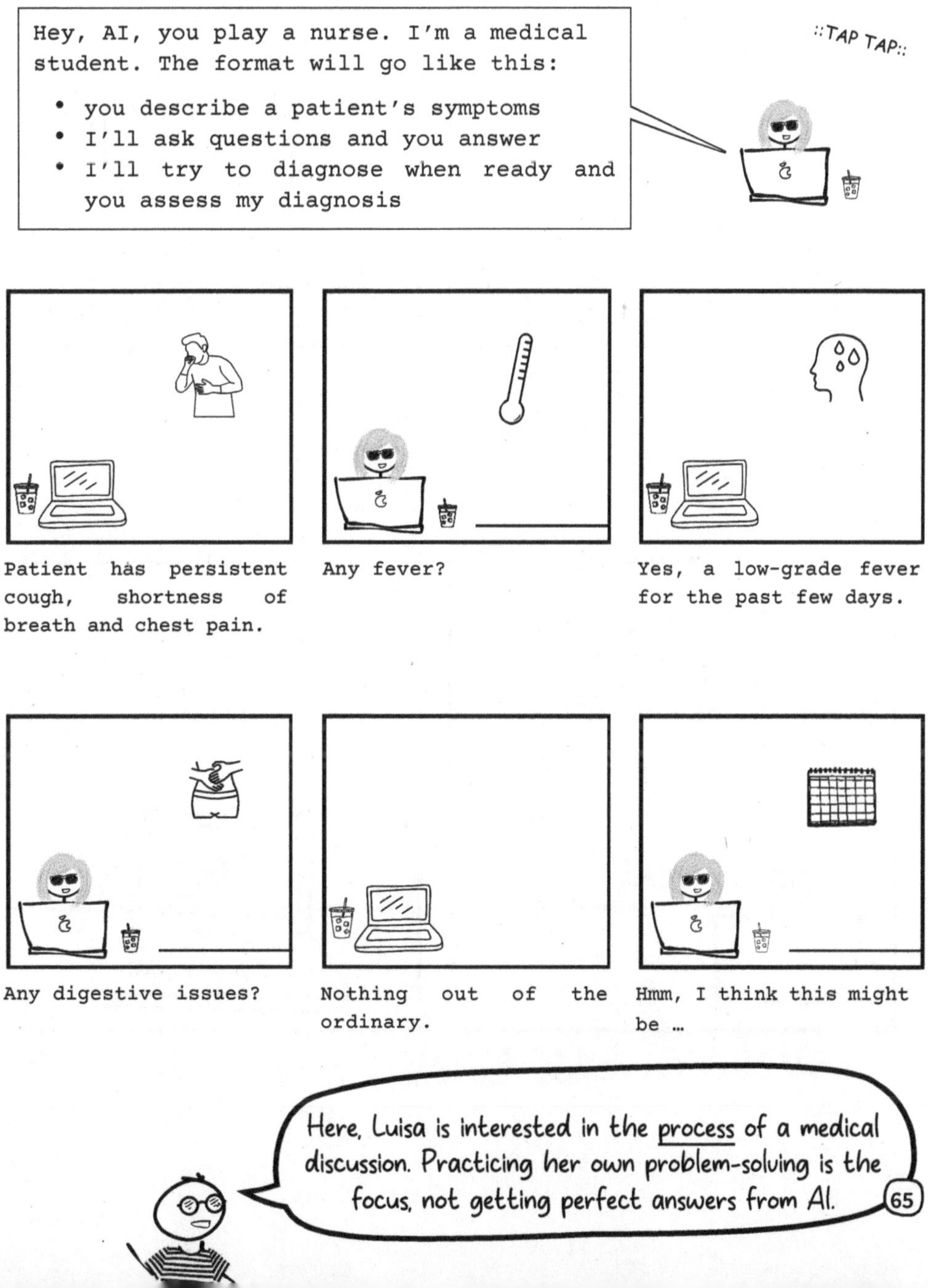

Hey, AI, you play a nurse. I'm a medical student. The format will go like this:
• you describe a patient's symptoms
• I'll ask questions and you answer
• I'll try to diagnose when ready and you assess my diagnosis
::TAP TAP::
Patient has persistent cough, shortness of breath and chest pain.
Any fever?
Yes, a low-grade fever for the past few days.
Any digestive issues?
Nothing out of the ordinary.
Hmm, I think this might be ...
Here, Luisa is interested in the process of a medical discussion. Practicing her own problem-solving is the focus, not getting perfect answers from AI.

4.1 Role play

You could have the AI play a character in a script for theatre …

Using only Walter's lines in the play *Raisin in the Sun*, answer my questions.
What is your biggest ambition?
::TAP TAP::
SCRIPT
'I want so many things that they are driving me kind of crazy … '

… or the bot plays a reporter in 2035 …

I'm a geopolitical analyst focused on geography & demographics. You're a journalist in 2035. Ask me about the future of Germany.
::TAP TAP::
NEWS
In what ways have new technologies and automation influenced the labour market in 2030s Germany?

… the possibilities are endless.

4.1 Role play

Remember that the bot might fabricate quotations or point you in directions that aren't always helpful. If you keep that in mind, you can design **ARF**-style interactions that aren't focused on getting 100% good answers from the bot. Instead, you'll focus on giving **your own brain** a workout.

The point is to find ways for you to work actively and to enjoy practising. It's about developing your own discursive skills, not getting magic answers from a genie in a lamp.

For example, if you want to train yourself to participate more in class or ask more questions in lecture, this is a great way to practise.

Now let's look at how discussion-style approaches can work to brainstorm and generate ideas.

Let's get my friend Khari to join us. Are you ready, Khari?
Yeah, let's go!

4.2 Brainstorm

As always, tell the AI chatbot what you want to do and how you want to do it. For example, maybe you have lots of ideas for an essay but don't know where to start or how to structure the text. Try using the chatbot to sort this out.

ARF

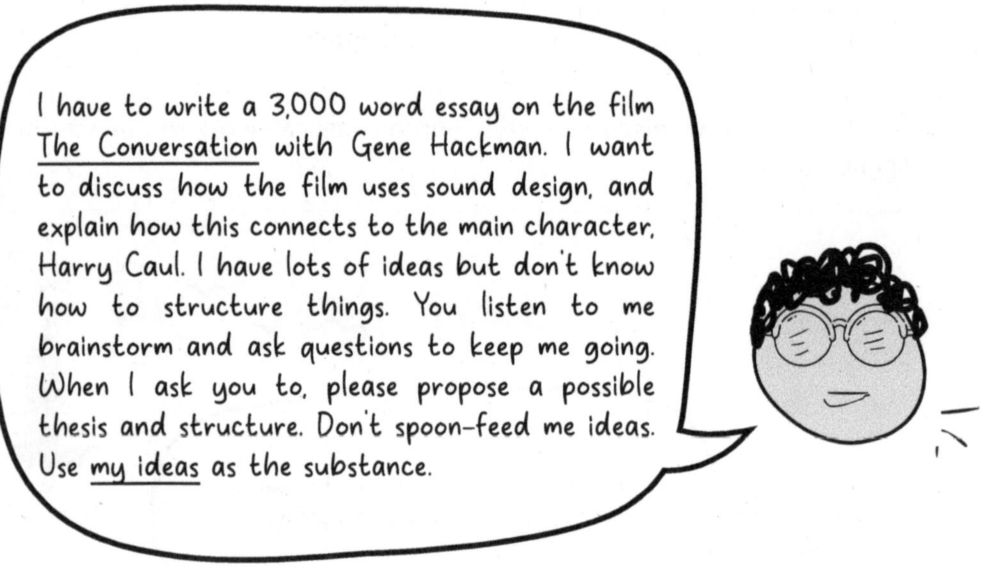
I have to write a 3,000 word essay on the film The Conversation with Gene Hackman. I want to discuss how the film uses sound design, and explain how this connects to the main character, Harry Caul. I have lots of ideas but don't know how to structure things. You listen to me brainstorm and ask questions to keep me going. When I ask you to, please propose a possible thesis and structure. Don't spoon-feed me ideas. Use my ideas as the substance.

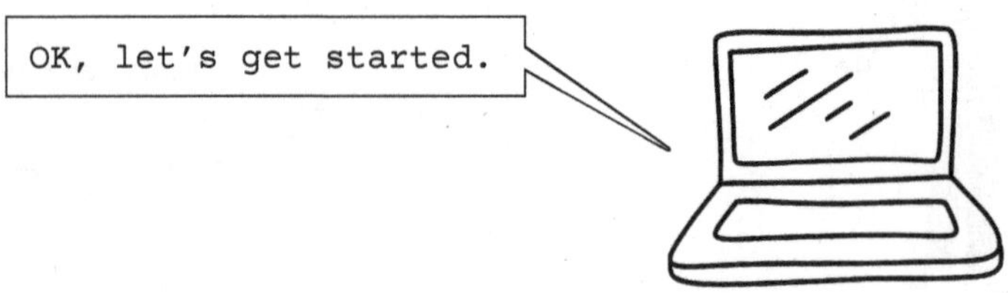
OK, let's get started.

4.2 Brainstorm

Well, I think it's all about privacy. Harry Caul is a surveillance expert and he specializes in innovative ways to place listening devices to record audio secretly. But he's obsessed with his own privacy.
How does the film's sound design show Caul's obsession with privacy? Can you give specific examples?
He keeps seeing his girlfriend in secret. I think he wants to protect her. He gets all paranoid when he hears her sing a song that someone else was singing. He keeps playing saxophone alone in his apartment.
Let's see ... there are both public soundscapes and private ones, and the private ones are often solo voices and solo instruments, whereas the public ones are often broad soundscapes with lots going on and people talking and interference and the sounds of the city ... . It feels like kind of post-war high modernism tension with like the alienation of the city and some anxiety about the rate of change in cities and in technology, I guess?
... So are you, like, getting some sort of sense of my interests?

4.2 Brainstorm

Absolutely. You've noted a few key aspects we could chat more about:

1. Private vs. public soundscapes: How do they mirror Caul's mental state and his professional life?
2. Repeated sounds: What significance does the repetition of the song his girlfriend sings hold …
3. Societal anxiety …

Repetition, that's interesting. Let's talk more about how many times the song 'Red Red Robin' repeats and how it's expressed in different parts of the film.

Sure. Tell me more about that song and how it is treated in the film.

LATER THAT DAY ...

Hey, Josh, I just talked with gen AI for ten mins and worked out an outline for my essay.
Isn't that, like, cheating or something?
No, it used all my ideas. It just grouped them into themes.
Oh. So you're putting all those ideas in the essay?
Not all of them. The process helped me focus on a topic I can manage.
Nice one! Sounds like you're making good use of the tech, without becoming fully reliant on it.

Thanks – I'm trying to keep a good balance.
What about criticality?
Yeah, criticality is cool.
I mean, can you use the bot to help you think critically?
Oh, right. Yeah, I could get it to play devil's advocate or something.
Yeah, those lecturers are always banging on about critical thinking, eh?

Pause: Reassess as you go

Remember, gen AI is not a reliable 'source of truth'. It's not a stable knowledge base (like an encyclopaedia might be). It's an engine designed to give you an answer that's statistically likely to serve your purpose. That's not the same as telling you the truth.

Imagine you ask a chatbot for a list of 'top twenty articles from the past five years on indigenous views on community'. It may 'hallucinate' some of the answer. It may not understand what you mean by 'top' or 'community' or which indigenous cultures you're interested in. And it will likely have a western-biased interpretation of those cultures.

So, whenever you interact with a gen AI chatbot, pause often to assess several things:

Accuracy: Are you getting correct information? Cross-check against a reliable source before you trust AI's outputs.

Relevance: Is the AI 'getting it'? Is it responding with the context and detail you need? If not, you can iterate your prompt. Or even better, balance your use of AI by interacting with journals, books and ... real people!

Sycophancy: Is the bot challenging you enough or is it simply telling you what you want to hear? What will your response be?

Bias: Don't forget, gen AI is trained largely on the internet, and the internet has all kinds of biases about right and wrong, interesting and uninteresting, true and false. What is the bot not seeing?

Learning and well-being: Is your AI interaction good for you as a learner? Does it feel good as a person? Is it helping you to thrive ... or draining your brain?

Ask a chatbot to respond to your unedited ideas and give you follow-up questions. Be clear about the type of support you want.

Once you've developed the idea in a way that's useful for your learning, take a break from the chatbot. Perhaps use a scrap of paper or talk to a friend. Perhaps sketch out some ways to structure your ideas or make a plan for pushing the project further. After this time away from AI, you might return to it and ask the bot for feedback.

~

What did you think? Is this a helpful way to generate ideas? Does it help you keep on top of things and get more organized? Do you ever feel misled or overwhelmed with ideas?

Pay attention to the experience of using the technology and adjust as you go.

4.3 Test your arguments

Ask the AI chatbot to help you test your arguments and think critically* about your own ideas. Here are a few examples. You can ask the chatbot to:

- play 'devil's advocate' – argue against you, test your logic
- give another perspective – show you views you haven't considered
- generate counterfactuals – pose 'what if' scenarios to stress-test your conclusions
- find your assumptions – call you out on assumptions that could be affecting your objectivity
- clarify definitions – push you to define the terms of your argument

And there are many other ways to experiment with criticality. These can help you strengthen your argument or even change your mind about what you believe.

Hey, chatbot, point out assumptions in my argument:
Students using academic support services get higher grades. This proves these services have a positive impact on student performance.
The statistic shows a correlation, but you haven't provided further evidence to indicate a cause-effect relationship.
Oh, OK. I think the study had a control group I should mention. I'll go back and check.

* Here, critical thinking means to consider lots of possibilities and make careful assessments of ideas.

4.3 Test your arguments

Here's another example:

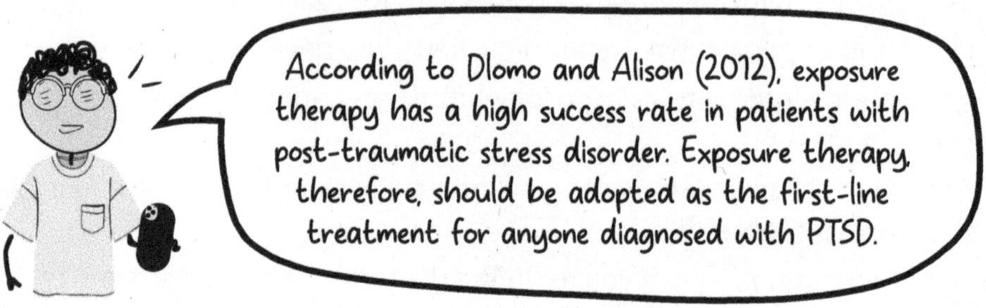
According to Dlomo and Alison (2012), exposure therapy has a high success rate in patients with post-traumatic stress disorder. Exposure therapy, therefore, should be adopted as the first-line treatment for anyone diagnosed with PTSD.

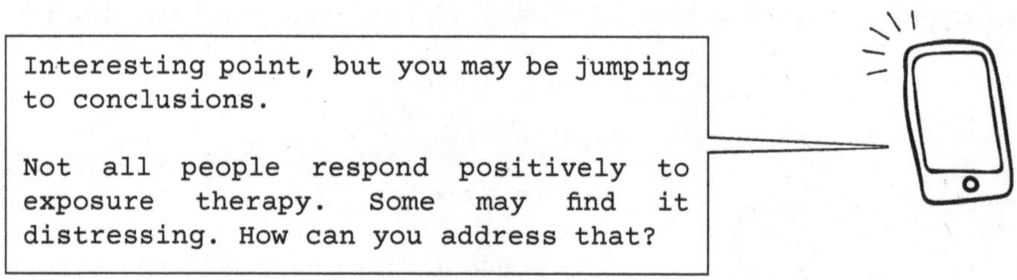
Interesting point, but you may be jumping to conclusions.
Not all people respond positively to exposure therapy. Some may find it distressing. How can you address that?

4.3 Test your arguments

Shoot, now I have to change my whole argument – what a waste of time!
Don't give up, Khari! It's OK to spot a complication in your argument, just be sure to address it in your writing.
Oh, OK, that doesn't sound too bad, I guess.
Yeah. In fact, your teachers will probably like it.
Like it, eh? ...

4.3 Test your arguments

Great, I'll just cut and paste the chatbot's line right in there then ...
– CLIK –
– PASTE –
Not all people respond positively to exposure therapy ...
This is awesome. All the time I'm saving will let me to get back to gaming, ASAP!

Hold up there, pal.

Just cutting and pasting from the bot will almost certainly be considered poor academic practice ... or worse, plagiarism.

You could get in trouble with a bunch of grumpy academics!

Anyway, what about the whole idea that the best use of these tools is not to get easy answers, but to make you think and help you learn more?

Right, right, right, OK. So, what should I do instead?
Why not search the research literature to follow up this idea?
Yeah, I could really get into it if I find some good research articles!

Pause: Document your process

To support your learning *and* keep you on the right side of academic integrity, consider keeping a process portfolio.

You simply document as much of your rough work as possible and keep it ready. Then, if your teachers worry you've used too much AI, you've got a folder of stuff you can point to and show them the work you've done.

Take pics of your napkin sketches and brainstorming notes, keep old drafts of writing saved as different versions, make screenshots of library searches, take audio memos as you work through your ideas, keep a log of every activity that's gone into doing the work … be creative.

This builds evidence to show your teachers how hard you worked, but it also makes you more focused on your working process and gives you an excuse to try different approaches to active learning.

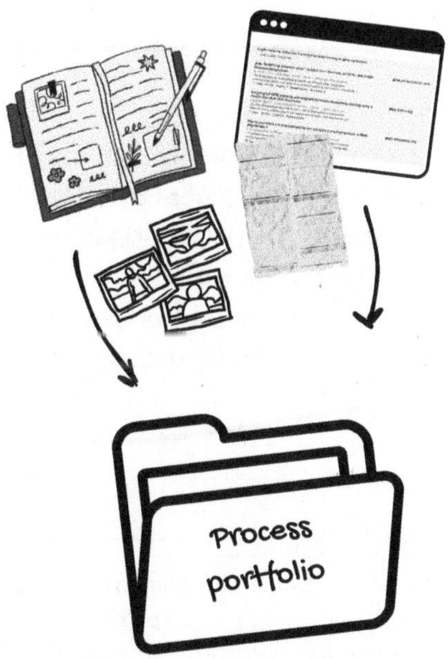

4.4 Think critically

In many learning environments, critical thinking is a constant demand. A lot of people find this difficult. It can feel kind of scary, like taking a risk, or just making your brain do a lot of things at once.

Many educators are so comfortable with critical thinking, they've forgotten it's difficult to learn. They've forgotten that students sometimes feel vulnerable when they try to practise this skill. The good news: it *can* be practised, with AI or other people, and it gets less scary.

So, ask an AI bot to help you practice your critical thinking skills. Get it to give you prompts that you have to respond to. Ask it to assess your critique and push you to develop the idea further.

ARF

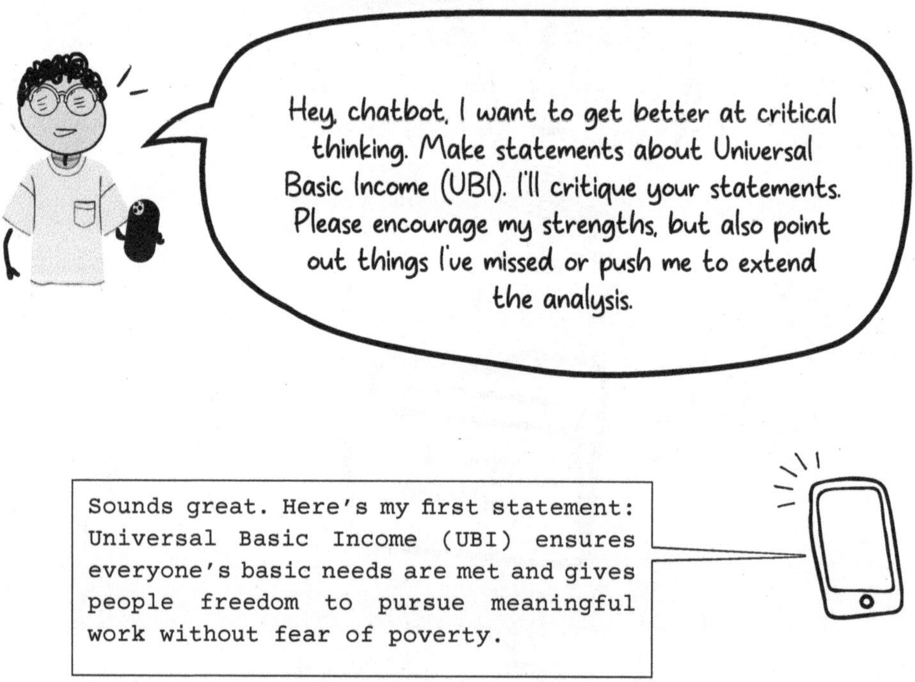
Hey, chatbot, I want to get better at critical thinking. Make statements about Universal Basic Income (UBI). I'll critique your statements. Please encourage my strengths, but also point out things I've missed or push me to extend the analysis.
Sounds great. Here's my first statement: Universal Basic Income (UBI) ensures everyone's basic needs are met and gives people freedom to pursue meaningful work without fear of poverty.

4.4 Think critically

This argument assumes that 'basic needs' can be met by money alone. Show me the evidence.
Good point. Evidence is important. Can you suggest an alternative framing of 'basic needs'?
Sure: having fun and connecting socially.
You're nailing this!
Oh, chatbot, please don't be so sycophantic ... challenge me!
My bad!

4.4 Think critically

How come you guys are being, like, so polite to these chatbots? Isn't that of kind silly, to treat a machine like a human?
It is a bit strange. That's called anthropomorphism. When we treat non-humans like humans.
However, for me, since the platforms are designed this way, I tend to go along with it because it's an easy way of working.

In fact, some evidence shows that being polite to chatbots gets better results. And some say that being polite just feels better as an experience.
But there are problems and risks associated with this. Bots are designed to seem human but they aren't. We shouldn't treat them as friends.
Yeah, because chatbots don't have feelings, right? I mean, they're not conscious beings.

We have no reason to think they are any more conscious than other computer systems.
But the strange truth is:
a) we don't know how consciousness happens, and
b) we have no sure-fire way to prove whether something is or isn't.
So, you mean we could create a conscious bot and not even know it?

4.4 Think critically

That's right. And even if we tell ourselves rationally that we doubt these machines are conscious, it sometimes feels like they are alive, like they have feelings.
And some people are already behaving as if AIs are conscious. Some people have fallen in love with AIs or become dangerously dependent on their conversations with bots.
Whoa! That's a reason to be really self-aware and cautious when using AI technologies.

4.4 Think critically

Use a chatbot to critique and challenge an idea or argument you are working on or have heard from others. Does it lead you to discover new and interesting perspectives? Or does the bot simply praise your ideas and make you feel like a genius? A bit of both?

Next, practice your own ability to think critically. Ask a bot to present you with a flawed argument so you can practice finding the limitations, assumptions, problems or nuances of an idea.

Wait! Don't stop there ... find the next step. If you discover a new perspective through working with a chatbot, great. But can you then find an author or researcher connected to that idea? Can you find literature? Chatting with bots is not a replacement for reading articles and books, discussing with humans and getting involved in your field of study.

~

Does this activity help you get a feel for how critical discussion goes?

Pause: AI literacy (part II)

So, are you becoming more critically **AI literate**? Do you have a feel for how AI systems work and what their strengths and weaknesses are? Do you have a sense of the trade-off you make between autonomy and automation?

By now, I hope you have had a chance to practise:

- **assessing if and when** AI tools are useful or appropriate,
- **making clear intentions** when working with AI,
- **designing skilful prompts** and **interactions** that support your learning,
- **critiquing** AI's outputs for quality, bias, sycophancy and other issues, and
- **reflecting** on your own habits and experiences with AI ... as well as the effects the tech has on you, your education and society as a whole.

In what ways is gen AI positive or negative for your learning and well-being? What approach will you take moving forward?

5. Find sources and key ideas in a field

Ask the chatbot to help you find useful sources or get you 'up to speed' on a certain topic. As always, specify what you're looking for and how you want to interact. It can also help to specify that you only want real, scholarly sources.

In point form and less than 100 words, teach me about key debates around solar energy's sustainability. Provide a real scholarly source for each topic area (maximum ten years old).

- Lithium Availability: Debates over limited lithium reserves for battery production impacting long-term sustainability (NREL, Annual Technology Baseline, 2021).
- Environmental Impact: Mining for materials like lithium and silicon can harm ecosystems (Hernandez et al., Nature Sustainability, 2019).
- Recycling Challenges …

5. Find sources and key ideas in a field

Remember, don't assume the LLM's sources are accurate. Go search for them yourself to confirm they exist and verify they say what the bot says they say.
Understood. But let's keep digging here. Chatbot, can you recommend an article that looks at a few energy alternatives and how they might work together to help decarbonize energy?
Sure! In 'Deep Decarbonization of the Electric Power Sector' (2020), Jenkins & Thernstrom examine various pathways for decarbonization. They argue that …
!!

5. Find sources and key ideas in a field

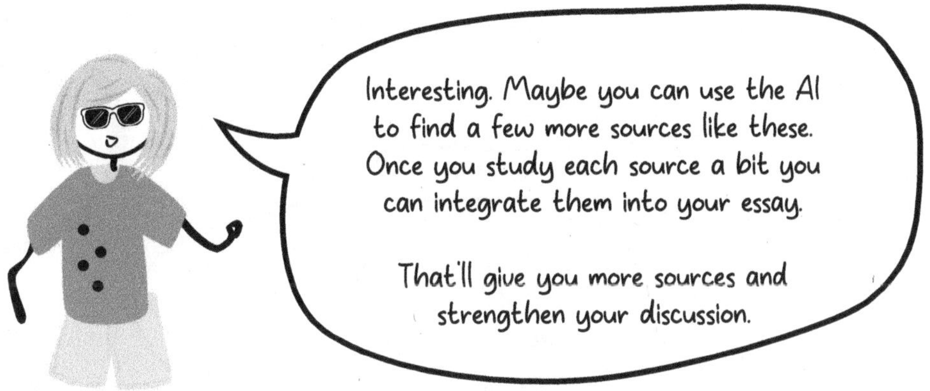
Interesting. Maybe you can use the AI to find a few more sources like these. Once you study each source a bit you can integrate them into your essay.
That'll give you more sources and strengthen your discussion.

That actually sounds pretty interesting.
And it's a fast way to get started. After that I can spend more time with my library's research databases, homing in on more texts.

5. Find sources and key ideas in a field

That's right. Don't stop searching the library databases. That can yield really good results, whereas AI tools don't always find the most suitable stuff.
In fact, Khari, try using a chatbot to come up with more keyword phrases to search for at your library.
OK, chatbot, I have to do research on leadership models in sport.
I've searched 'alternative leadership' and 'leading by example', but I'm not getting much.
Suggest a few others.
OK, try these:
1. Transformational leadership
2. Authentic leadership
3. …

5. Find sources and key ideas in a field

Nice one. You know, I've been tempted to use the tools to simply spit out a dozen sources and throw them into my references section.
But I felt kind of lousy doing that. The only thing I learned was how to cut and paste!
Yeah, you're probably spending a lot of time and money studying, right? So you have to think carefully about what the bot does for you, and what you take on yourself. Don't waste the opportunity to grow!
I get it.
To be honest, I'd find it kind of boring just letting the tools do all the work.

5. Find sources and key ideas in a field

Exactly.
And by the way, when AI gives you a summary of a text, don't assume you've now learned that idea and you're done. Treat an AI summary like the blurb on the back of a book: just a start.
It helps you decide whether to read further and figure out what you're looking for when you do read more. An AI summary, after all, is solving a problem for you ... it removes the rich challenge that reading a full text can give you. Don't stop reading!
Can't I just quote the AI tool and cite it like I would any source of information?
Technically you could. But your teachers probably won't consider that a good source. In any case, you'll want to a) do it for a good reason and b) follow your teachers' guidelines.

5. Find sources and key ideas in a field

Let's say your teachers asked you to reflect on and critique the output of an LLM. You might then write something like the following example ...
AI essay by Josh Thorpe
When prompted to tell a joke in the style of Rodney Dangerfield, ChatbotX replied, 'I got a self-driving car. It sees me coming and drives away! I tell ya, I get no respect' (ChatbotX, 2025). See Appendix 1 for a full transcript of the chat.
... Always using the citation style your teachers ask for.
But citing chatbots is not like citing other sources. And for most things, your teachers will likely prefer scholarly, human sources. In the same way Wikipedia is not often considered fully reliable, neither are chatbots.

5. Find sources and key ideas in a field

Also, your institution might ask you to make some kind of statement whenever you hand in an assignment.
COVER SHEET FOR ESSAYS
I used AI tools to write my paper for me
I used AI tools to find readings, brainstorm and plan
I did not use AI tools
Some assignments may ask you not to use AI tools at all, while others might encourage you to use the tools in specific ways.
See the next page on the AIAS for more on this ...

Pause: The AI Assessment Scale

Many educators are using a tool called the AI Assessment Scale (AIAS) to guide how you use gen AI in your work. Your teachers might ask you to use the AIAS to guide your decisions when doing different assignments. And they might ask you to make a declaration indicating your work conforms to their stated expectations. The AIAS has five levels, ranging from no AI at all to AI 'exploration'.

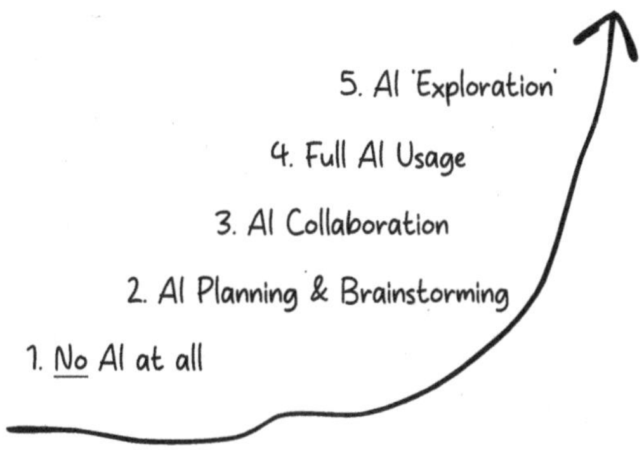

The AIAS is short-hand for agreeing broadly on how you use AI in assignments. But it doesn't say much about whether or how your use of AI is or is not good for your learning. So, if your teachers use the AIAS, you should still reflect on all the stuff this book is asking you to reflect on. Like, is this good for me? Am I using my own brain or outsourcing my intelligence?

5.1 Analyse sources

Here's a cool thing you might not have thought of using gen AI for: to do a kind of first-step analysis to reveal formal characteristics of long texts. This can be a fast way to view a text from a technical view, so you can then consider and critique it more closely.

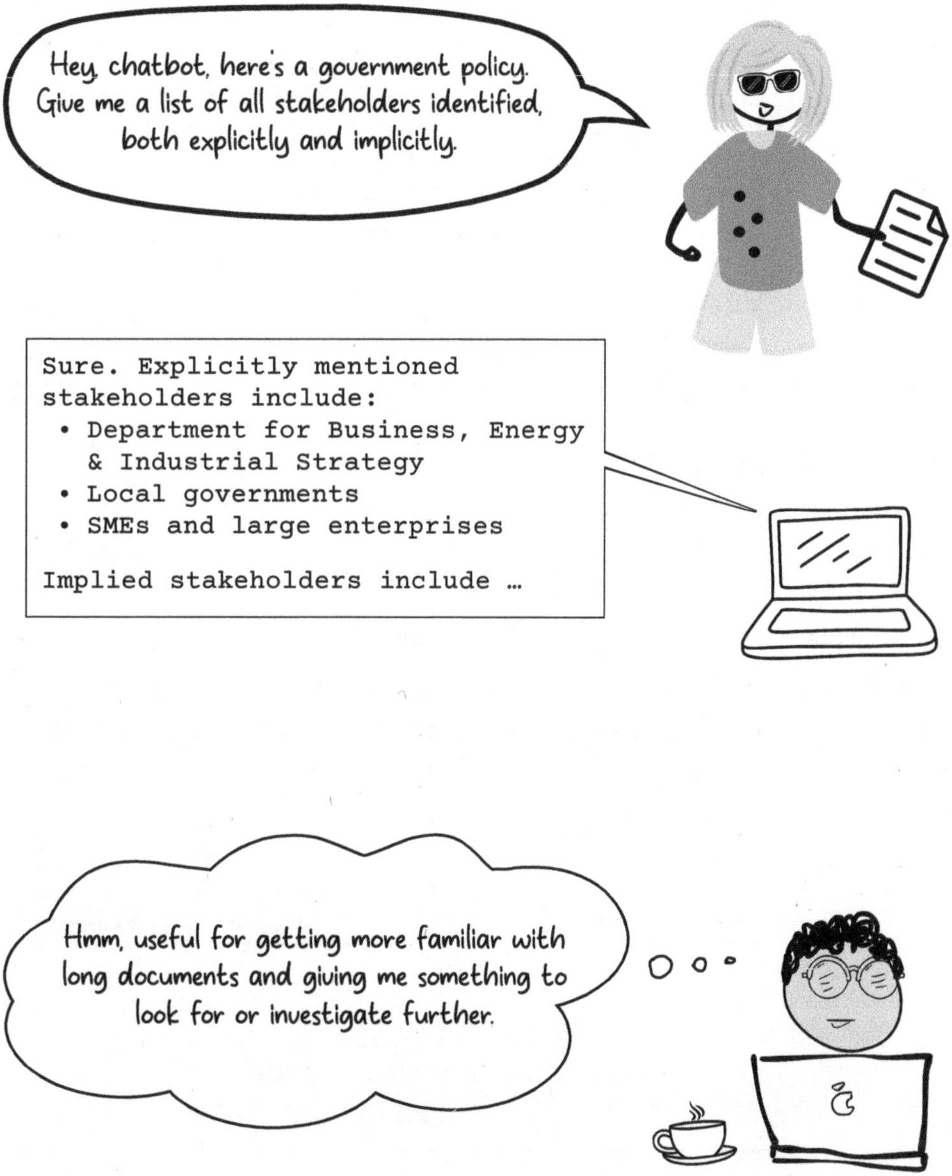

Hey, chatbot, here's a government policy. Give me a list of all stakeholders identified, both explicitly and implicitly.
Sure. Explicitly mentioned stakeholders include:
• Department for Business, Energy & Industrial Strategy
• Local governments
• SMEs and large enterprises
Implied stakeholders include ...
Hmm, useful for getting more familiar with long documents and giving me something to look for or investigate further.

Hey, chatbot, in that document do you see any uses of language that suggest bias from the Government's perspective?
In this document, businesses are often framed through active, positive terms like 'innovator' or 'opportunity'. But unions and non-profits are more frequently described with language that suggests passivity and difficulty, such as 'obstacle' or 'challenge'.
Super interesting. I'll look more closely at the text and pick it apart. Maybe I can do some interesting rhetorical analysis!
Definitely look more closely. Chatbots can give you a great start. After that, dig in, learn more, develop and refine.

Pause: Deepfakes, slop and bullshit

Deepfakes are AI-generated fictions that masquerade as reality. Have you ever seen a video online and weren't sure whether it was real or not? Have you ever known anyone who used AI-generated images of someone else in unfair or bullying ways? Sounds like a deepfake.

Deepfakes are radically challenging our sense of what's real. As this becomes more common, we may find it harder to trust digital information. We'll have to pay close attention to our media diet. It may mean we depend more and more on digital gatekeepers and traditional news sources like big newspapers.

Slop is AI-generated, low-quality content designed as filler or clickbait. We've always had garbage content but it was never so easy and quick to spew out. Is that the kind of information environment you want to live in?

Bullshit, according to philosopher Harry G. Frankfurt, is speech or writing that is neither truth nor lie – speech or writing which is *indifferent* to truth.

Imagine a few blokes blowing off steam in a pub, not really caring whether what they say is true or not. This is bullshit as Frankfurt means it. In some cases it's harmless and serves a purpose (part of having a laugh at the pub).

But sometimes it's harmful, like when political leaders invent controversial fictions to deceive or enrage people. This can be dangerous.

Now think about gen AI. Its main aim is to give a response to satisfy your demand for an answer. As far as we know, it has no moral or ethical obligation to the truth. It's a bit like bullshit, is it not? Does that concern you?

But if you use gen AI as this book advocates, as a space to strengthen your own thinking, it is less important just how true the bot's statements are. If you're using gen AI to **think more, not less**, you're not relying on AI for content so much. You're using it as a space to practice your own knowledge and thinking processes.

6. Ace your assessments

There are all kinds of assessments. And gen AI has prompted many educators to move on from standard assignments like essays and reports. Today the focus is often shifting to group work, field work, practical skills or various processes you document in a portfolio. My **think more, not less** approach should work well for all of the above.

Assignments used to feel like this:

Lately, we're doing a bit more of this:

6. Ace your assessments

Understanding and responding to the wide range of assessments is a skill in itself.

Your teachers will often give you loads of instructions, rubrics, tips, pdfs, weblinks and other extras for every assignment. It can be helpful, but you might also feel a bit confused by it all. It's no surprise that people often lose track.

Try to bring it all together and make your own **one-page brief**. This can help you become really familiar with the assignment. I'd recommend trying this without AI. Speak to your teachers and participate in seminars – these are often the best ways to engage with assessments.

If you struggle to manage all this, however, **gen AI could help**. Try uploading the related assignment documents to a chatbot and asking for help to clarify the whole range of advice better.

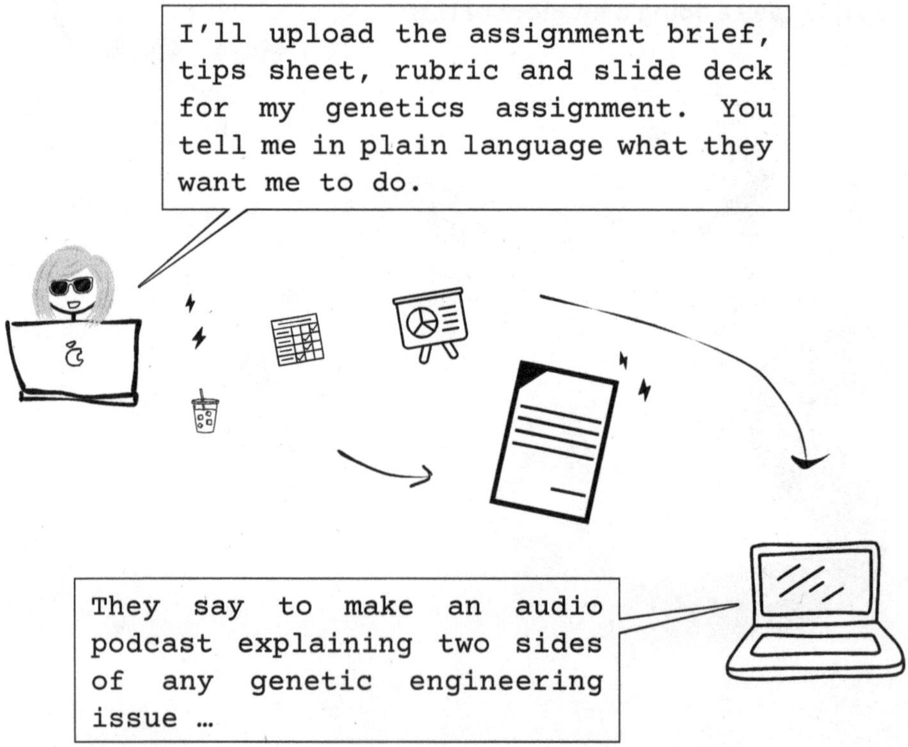
I'll upload the assignment brief, tips sheet, rubric and slide deck for my genetics assignment. You tell me in plain language what they want me to do.
They say to make an audio podcast explaining two sides of any genetic engineering issue …

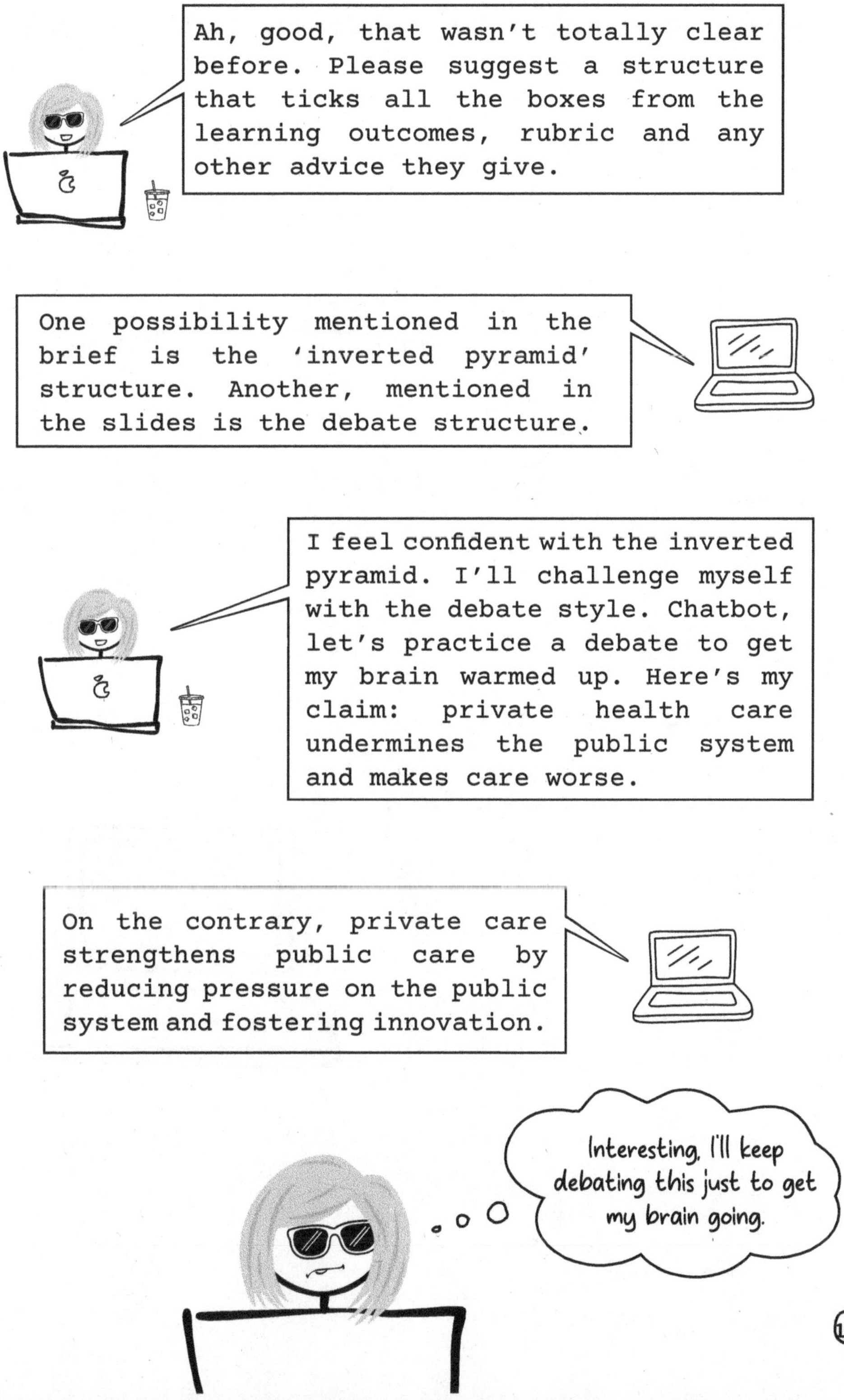
Ah, good, that wasn't totally clear before. Please suggest a structure that ticks all the boxes from the learning outcomes, rubric and any other advice they give.
One possibility mentioned in the brief is the 'inverted pyramid' structure. Another, mentioned in the slides is the debate structure.
I feel confident with the inverted pyramid. I'll challenge myself with the debate style. Chatbot, let's practice a debate to get my brain warmed up. Here's my claim: private health care undermines the public system and makes care worse.
On the contrary, private care strengthens public care by reducing pressure on the public system and fostering innovation.
Interesting, I'll keep debating this just to get my brain going.

6.1 Transcribe your ideas

Are you the kind of person who likes to talk ideas out, like Khari did earlier? You can try dictating to a chatbot and have it transcribe and organize your ideas.

As always, use ARF to tell the bot what you want to do and how you want it to do it.

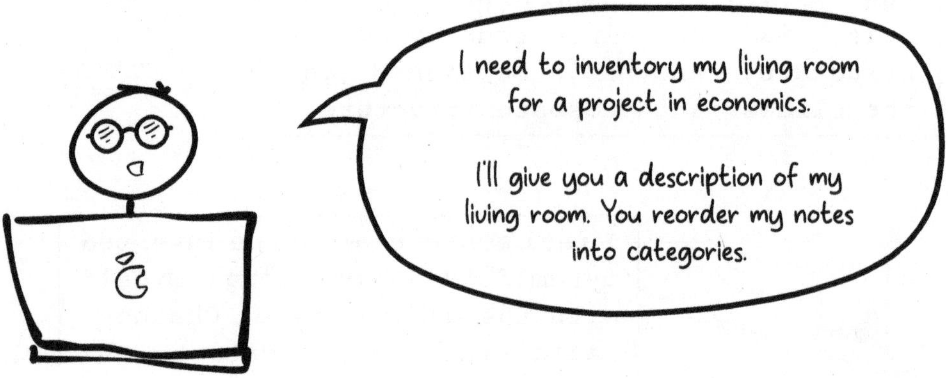
I need to inventory my living room for a project in economics.
I'll give you a description of my living room. You reorder my notes into categories.

Are there any special categories you'd like me to use?

6.1 Transcribe your ideas

Furniture, plants, appliances and anything else you recommend. OK, here we go:
So the room I'm in is about 120 sq ft, um, six different plants in it, a spider plant, a kind of nettle, a coffee table, an orchid, a couple of cactuses, something I don't know what it is ...

—SEVERAL MINUTES PASS—

Here's your room sorted into categories:

<u>Furniture</u>
- table and two chairs
- bookshelves (5)
- TV unit
- small coffee table (marble and wood)
- ...

<u>Plants</u>
- spider plant
- nettle
- orchid
- cactuses (2)
- unknown plant
- ...

<u>Appliances</u>
- TV
- ...

[etc].

6.1 Transcribe your ideas

OK, now I have to analyse my own habits as a consumer of plants.
I've heard about an idea in economics, like ... as you have more and more of something its value to you may decrease.
Is there a word for that?
You're describing the concept of 'marginal utility'. Marginal utility is ...

Wow, that's useful!
It seems like you could have some pretty productive chats with these bots.
Yeah – you could think of a bot as an assistant, a peer-tutor or even a 'reverse dictionary'. But remember, at least for now, don't trust the output of bots too much. They have no moral obligation to the truth.

6.2 Plan

You can ask an AI tool to help you plan an essay, a piece of writing, a presentation or some other project. Planning ahead can help you produce stronger work and it often helps to reduce stress because you feel more in control and settled.

Important note: don't try to make a perfect plan, and don't feel bad if you don't stick to the plan. The real value of planning is to give you the mental space to do your work ... and to be flexible when the unexpected occurs.

Hey, chatbot, I have an idea for a book that helps students use AI tools most effectively. Listen to my notes and suggest a point-form structure with sub-points I can follow.
Don't add any new ideas, just use my ideas. I'm just not sure the best order or how to put things in categories and sub-categories.
OK, I can help with that.

6.2 Plan

OK, so here goes. The book wants to coach students on using the tools and basically on being good 'prompt designers' for learning. It wants to get across that the most exciting use of AI tools in education is how they can give students opportunities to use their brains more, not less ...
Let's see ... main sections I thought about putting in were: having conversations to do critical thinking, exploring and understanding concepts, brainstorming, plan writing, role playing ... and then also more straightforward stuff like practice for exams, processing notes, transcribing dictation ... Oh, and also some thoughts in general on critical digital literacy (using all digital media more reflectively). Um, there will also be some general tips about good study practice sprinkled throughout.
OK, please suggest a logical structure in a numbered, nested list.
...

6.2 Plan

OK, here's a structure you can follow:

1. Introduction
   - Purpose of the Book
   - The Role of AI Tools in Enhancing Education
   - Emphasizing Brain Engagement Over Automation
2. Understanding AI Tools
   - Overview of AI in Education
   - Benefits and Limitations
   - Ethical Considerations: Brief Discussion on Plagiarism
3. etc …*

Wait wait, wait …

* Excerpt adapted from ChatGPT.

6.2 Plan

That's not quite right. You didn't capture my style. I'm not writing an academic book. It's more of a fun and practical book. Students need to jump straight in and start trying things out.

Also, the order should reflect roughly the order people might follow when they're first thinking about their academic skills. Like they might start with lectures and stuff. Try again, OK?

I see, let's try this:

1. Getting Started With AI Tools
   - Introduction to AI in Education
   - Setting Up Your AI Tools
   - Basic Tips for Effective Use
2. Basic Applications for First-Year Students
   - Using AI for Exam Practice
   - Organizing and Understanding Lecture Notes
   - Transcribing and Reworking Dictation
3. etc …*

* Excerpt adapted from ChatGPT.

6.2 Plan

That's getting closer, but I think I'll have to keep working on it myself. Maybe get some feedback from a friend or peer editor. I won't use some of those suggestions.
But thanks, chatbot, this has helped me get started on something I was putting off.
Don't mention it.
Now, let's see if you can help me plan how to do the project itself and put everything in my calendar.

6.2 Plan

So ... I need to brainstorm some ideas first, and document all of them somehow. Suggest three ways. Then I should do some research on prompt engineering. Suggest five scholarly sources on this topic. Then I need to start creating the visual style and characters, then I start drafting, then editing, and then production for publication. My deadline is 1 Sept and I have two hours per day Mon–Thurs and six hours Fri–Sun.
Can you suggest a weekly project plan with things broken into one-hour chunks? (It's OK to have the same chunk repeated one after the other sometimes.)

6.2 Plan

Week 1: Brainstorming and Documentation

- 1–7 April
    - Monday: Brainstorm ideas (2 hours)
    - Tuesday: Brainstorm ideas (2 hours)
    - Wednesday: Organize and document ideas (2 hours)
    - Thursday: Organize and document ideas (2 hours)
    - Friday: Research prompt engineering (2 hours)
    - Saturday: Research prompt engineering (2 hours), summarize findings (2 hours)

Week 2: …*

Hmm, good start. But I see you didn't catch everything I mentioned and the timings are not totally realistic or entirely correct. I'll tweak it.
Can you show me how this would look as a Gantt chart?

* Excerpt adapted from ChatGPT.

6.2 Plan

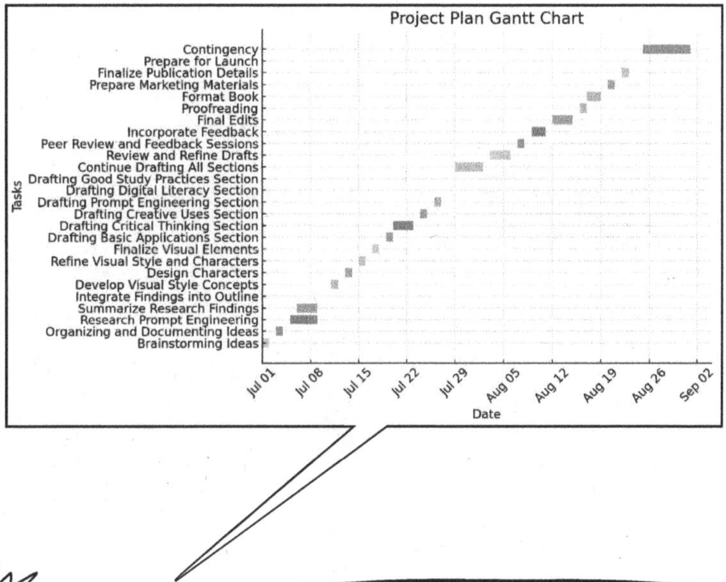

*

* Gantt chart generated by ChatGPT.

Week 5:
• Xyz...
I'll just make these timings more realistic ... add a few more tasks ... leave space for flexibility ...
Hmm, make a few more adjustments ...
S M T W T F S

Seems like you might have to do that one on your own, bro.
Well, if I spend longer coaching the bot I'll probably coax a final plan from it.
The point is, you have to put in good ideas to get good ideas out ... and be willing to experiment and not accept everything the bot gives you.
I think of this process as 'rapid prototyping'. You know – to get a rough idea quickly, and then refine it.
It's all part of an approach I think of as AI minimalism. Just use it a little. And I'll tell you more about that later ...
You know what, with all this thinking, I might need a break soon.

6.2 Plan

Hey, Josh, do you feel a slightly uncomfortable feeling of effort?
Hmm, indeed I do.
That could be the feeling of learning. Try to embrace that!
Haha, OK, I can handle that.
CLAP
CLAP

6.2 Plan

Try using AI to interpret your assignment instructions, transcribe and organize your ideas, or plan an assignment. Think of the AI as a space to sort out the work, not as a one-stop solution.

~

How did you find this process? Do you feel the AI sped up the process? Made you more thorough? Reduced the cognitive load of doing assignments?

Pause: Is AI 'just a tool'?

People are fond of saying AI is 'just' a tool. Does that feel right to you? To me, it oversimplifies a very complex parasocial technology.

And I find people use this metaphor of the **tool** when they want to avoid thinking critically about the complex ways AI interacts with humans.

So, if it's not a tool, what is it?

Some people call AI an 'alien intelligence'.

Some call the conversations we have with chatbots 'parasocial relationships'.

Others like to think of AI as a system within a bigger system of knowledge exchange and emergent meaning …

As for me, I like to think of AI as a **virtual environment** or a **space for thinking** and learning. This spatial metaphor allows me to visualize myself interacting with AI and other technologies in lots of different ways. And I like to think that I could kind of rearrange the space depending on my aim that day.

What metaphor would you use to describe your experience with AI so far?

____

____

____

____

7. Write with AI

Have you ever been tempted to use a gen AI bot to write an entire essay for you?

Let's be honest, you could. The question is, should you?

Because you don't learn much that way. And teachers can't assess your actual knowledge and abilities that way. So it kind of undermines the validity of whatever learning or qualification you're aiming for. Which is a waste of time and money.

And it raises a question: do we have a responsibility to actually *have* the skills our qualifications we say we have?

I think so.

I mean, would you want to drive on a bridge built by an engineer who outsourced their master's thesis to a bot?

So, be clear on the rules and expectations of your teachers and mentors. Do they expect you to demonstrate your own knowledge and thinking in your writing? Have they been clear about how gen AI should or should not be used? Do you see how relying too much on gen AI robs you of some of the value of learning, and undermines the credibility of your qualifications?

But there's another reason to think carefully about this. It has to do with you as an individual – how you learn and create. I mean, what does writing mean to you? What purposes does it serve?

Let's try an experiment. As a little game, write a short sentence about the weather today. Two rules: **no AI helper** and **don't use the letter E**.

Challenging, right? And fun, I hope.

Now try asking a chatbot to do the same task.

What do you think of the bot's output versus your own? I'm guessing the vibe is a bit different.

What about the **experience** of writing the sentence versus the experience of having the chatbot do it?

For me, writing the sentence myself is a fun challenge that makes my brain work hard. I feel good afterward. But having a bot write the sentence feels boring. There's not much satisfaction.

How about you?

So, sometimes it matters that we do things ourselves. Sometimes the output itself is best coming from you, not a bot. And sometimes you want the experience of doing the thing, experiencing the process. And experience is something you simply cannot outsource.

What are some other reasons to limit your use of gen AI in writing?

Because I'm old-fashioned!

... because the writing process is a good challenge. It helps me figure things out and come up with novel ideas.

Or because I need to capture my personal perspective and style.
Or because I can write something more interesting than AI can.
Because I want to make sure I have a deep connection to what I need to learn.
Because my teacher wants me to, and I respect their trust.
Because it's just more fun.

Great! And yet, there are times when it truly doesn't matter who, or what, wrote the text.
Like the draft template for a small business contract. I can use lots of AI help there, review it, make changes, then show it to a lawyer for advice.
Unless, of course, I'm being assessed on the task and need to learn how to do it myself.
I think the key is to be clear on the rules.
And understand why the rules are there.
And know what I myself want to get out of the experience.

Speaking of the experience of writing, let's look a bit closer at different ways to look at writing. There are many ways. Writing can be:

A **process** you enjoy and which helps you **discover things** or **work out ideas**. In this case, you might try writing with no AI support. Give yourself the experience of this process of thinking and discovery. It can be fun and rewarding – and using AI as a 'content mill' cheats you out of all those benefits.

An **expression of your 'voice', personality or identity**. Again, you might want to limit your use of gen AI here. Gen AI tends to use a style that's supposed to sound 'neutral'. For this very reason, some teachers might start placing more value on your 'voice' in your assignments. Of course, not everyone has a clear feeling for what it means to have a 'voice' in writing. So, ask for support from your teachers on how to achieve this.

A **construction**. We can think of writing as a material process, like building a wall or baking a cake. In this case you might be less fussy about having a clear sense of authorship or voice. Maybe it's more about making selections or decisions about what the text should include, and the end result simply has to work.

With this approach, AI might fit in more comfortably. Our collective feeling for *what writing is* may evolve. In some situations it might seem really natural to think of writing as constructing, building or assembling.

In this model, you are not pretending to be an isolated genius author, you are simply one part in a bigger system of knowledge-making.

How does each of these views connect with your own experience of writing? Does looking at the process from different perspectives help you make decisions about how much to rely on gen AI?

When in doubt, remember my credo: **Think more, not less, with gen AI**.

For your writing, that means you use gen AI to spark your thinking, to challenge it, to understand your writing better, and to help you reach farther … not just to spit out mediocre slop that might get you a passing grade (or a fail).

Pause: AI hygiene and AI minimalism

AI hygiene is a subset of **digital hygiene**. It just means how you decide to relate to digital technologies in ways that feel relatively healthy. For example, limiting video games to certain hours of the day, removing certain apps from your devices or agreeing not to use your phone during dinner with loved ones.

You can take a similar approach to AI. Figure out how to curate your use of the AI platforms to support your own well-being – not undermine it.

AI minimalism: Use AI just a little. No more than necessary. After all, there are probably only a few good reasons to use AI in learning. Two that come to mind for me are:

- If it helps me learn stuff – like my brain is doing more, being more creative and feeling more active than if I didn't use AI.
- If it automates low-value tasks, things I don't need to do myself – which frees up time for me to focus on work that's really valuable to me or to the world.

That's mostly it.

And achieving those sorts of things doesn't necessarily require hours of screen time. You may find that a few seconds or a few minutes is enough. Then switch modes and go work on paper or take a walk. Or talk with another human.

Pause: Jobs and the future of humanity

Earlier, I mentioned that some companies have the explicit intention of automating ALL WORK. Imagine a world without work! What would that look like?

What meaning will we humans find for ourselves if everything we need is done by machines? Will we figure out a way to make highly equal societies? Will we solve climate change and cancer? Will we live beautiful lives … or will we simply waste away?

These are fascinating questions. They may not be answered for many years.

But even today, your world is being impacted. The way we write and read, how we automate tasks such as writing code, analysing data or searching for information – it's all changing. And the skills you need today aren't always the same skills you need tomorrow. In such a world, it might feel difficult to know what skills to pursue.

So, what should you do? Well, in addition to building your critical AI literacy and critical digital literacy, you can become more professionally **resilient**. That means you become more adaptive to change and able to learn new things.

And today is a good time to make sure you develop human-centric skills to round out what you can offer in work and life. Some of these skills might be:

- creativity and problem-solving
- ability to collaborate with, care for and organize with other humans and living beings
- complex judgement involving human values and ethics
- decision-making, project management, coordination, adaptive management and leadership

You have so much to offer. It's just important to stay tuned in to how life and work are changing … and how *you* may need to change too. Again, it's all about **resilience**, **adaptability**, **creativity** and the ability to continue to **learn and evolve**.

In other words, **think more, not less**.

Tip: All this is a great reason for you to take initiative and make your assignments more interesting for yourself.

Let's say you are given an essay on community arts. Why not use this as an excuse to go volunteer at a community arts organization? You'll get material for the essay AND work experience that matters.

In the AI era, this approach can make you more skilled and hireable. It can also help you build resilience as you take on a greater range of small but meaningful challenges. So, wherever possible, use assignments to investigate the world, put yourself in interesting situations and gain practical experience in things that matter.

8. Final words

Alright ... well, this has been really fun! And before I send you off to do your own work, I just wanted to suggest a quick reflection:
Wherever you are in your learning, there are reasons you're doing it, right? What are those reasons?
Maybe you just like learning. Maybe you want to change your life in some way. Or change the world. Make a positive impact.
What are the values that underpin all this? What do you believe in? What makes you feel good?

8. Final words

Write in here

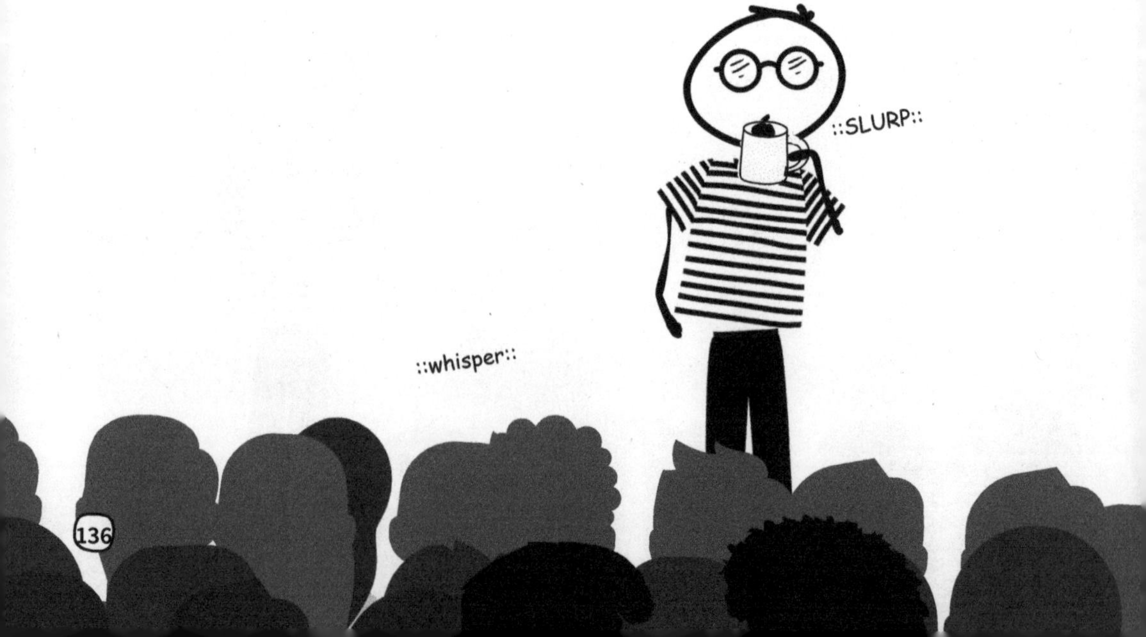
::SLURP::
::whisper::

8. Final words

Reaffirming your values and aims around learning is super useful any time. It's motivating and clarifying.
And clarifying your values and aims can help you decide when and how to use AI.
I mean, learning is about all kinds of challenges: new ideas, uncomfortable thoughts, new ways of doing things, curiosity, uncertainty, and lots of problems ...
Well, some problems are worth having. And some problems are worth owning – without the help of AI. Which ones? And how do you do it?
That's up to you.
CLAP
CLAP

8. Final words

Thanks guys, thanks. You know, writing this book, I've come to think as gen AI as a kind of distorting mirror.
See, culturally, these LLMs have hoovered up as much online human knowledge and culture as they could find. Looking into an LLM is like looking at a weird reflection of humanity. Why weird? Because it's biased and sycophantic and doesn't have a clear obligation to truth ... and all the other cautions we discussed.
Also, gen AI doesn't know human physical experience or emotion, so there are vast and important areas it simply can't reflect back to us. Written language is the main medium for working with chatbots, but that's just one way of knowing. All of knowledge, creativity, thinking – truth itself – is far more complicated than can be captured by an LLM.
For much of that, we have to look elsewhere.

On an individual level, too, gen AI can be compared to a mirror. Because a conversation with a chatbot is quite like a conversation with yourself. Especially if you adopt my credo: think more, not less, with gen AI.
If you're using the platforms this way, each interaction with an AI is also an encounter with yourself. A kind of self-portrait of your intuitions, your language, your ethics.
Go ahead and look at a conversation you've had with a bot. What drives, desires, fears, aims and assumptions can you uncover there? What does it show you about your intentions, feelings and views of the world? Kind of like a log of your interests and values.
If you look at it this way, at the end of the day, it really is true that the most interesting thing about AI is not AI ...

It's YOU!

8. Final words

8.1 What happens next?

I hope you've enjoyed the ride as much as I have! I've learned a lot. And if you're still reading, I hope you have too. But what happens next?

Well, the world is changing fast. Each of us will have to sort out for ourselves how to live in it. I mean, society is great at offering us lots of tech, but it isn't always good at showing us *how* to use technology in healthy ways. So, take care of yourselves ... and of each other. Learn to exercise careful **critical digital literacy** and **critical digital citizenry**. Take time to reflect on how these technologies impact your individual and collective lives. Let's work together to make thoughtful choices for a better world.

And, please, let's use these technologies only insofar as they make us more knowledgeable, creative and focused. So, if you ever start to feel unhappy or overwhelmed using AI tools, or if you feel they're dulling your wits, or making you lazy, or making you depressed, or desperate, or mean and unkind, or drawing you into anti-social behaviours ... it's time for a break. Have a talk with a real person. Go touch grass.

I think I'll do just that!

8.1 What happens next?

If you want to explore more tools and ideas, or to ask a question, please visit joshthorpe.com/ai. You can request my newsletter, find more useful tools and resources, or check out other writing and art.

And please **recommend** this book to your libraries, teachers, colleagues, friends and family. Or **review this book** on Amazon, Goodreads or anywhere reviews are read.

Post a pic of this book on socials and let people know you like it: #aiforstudents @thorpesstudio @bloomsburypublishing

Anyhow ... may you enjoy your intelligence, humans, whatever forms it may take.

Peace and well-being to you all!

Glossary

Academic integrity: Adhering to agreed expectations around authorship, giving credit where credit is due, and other assessed academic conduct within a learning environment

AIAS (Artificial Intelligence Assessment Scale): A framework for guiding the degree to which AI is allowed to be used for an assessment

AI critical literacy: The skillset of understanding how AI works, how to use it and how to reflect critically on the technology and your relation to it

AI vertigo: The feeling that the implications of AI, and the pace of change in the technology, is happening at a dizzying rate

Artificial intelligence (AI): Computing systems that are equal to or better than humans at **specific** aspects of knowledge work

Artificial general intelligence: Computing systems that are equal to or better than humans at **all** aspects of knowledge work

Artificial superintelligence: Computing systems that are **better than** humans at **all** aspects of knowledge work

Bias: A preference for one perspective over another that isn't based on evidence or fair reasoning

Booster: Someone who tends to highly optimistic, perhaps uncritical, views of a technology

Brain rot: Loss of cognitive ability (due to over-reliance on a technology)

Chatbot: A chat-based interface with a large language model

Colonial mindset: When a single corporation or culture assumes the right to exploit other people, cultures or resources

Consciousness: Sentience, awareness or the experience of having experience

Data privacy: Issues and rights surrounding what personal information is collected about you, how it's used and who can access it

Deepfake: An AI-generated simulation masquerading as the real thing

Doomer: Someone who tends to have highly pessimistic views of a technology

Glossary

Generative AI (gen AI): Technology that creates seemingly new content – like text, images or code – based on patterns learned from existing, largely human-generated, data

Hallucination: When gen AI invents things and makes statements that are not true

Intellectual property (IP): Legal ownership of writing, art, code, ideas, etc

Large language model (LLM): An AI system trained on massive amounts of text that can understand and generate human language

Plagiarism: When someone presents work as their own that they themselves did not in fact create

Prompt: Human input into a gen AI system

Prompt design/prompt engineering: Crafting skilful prompts for gen AI to produce a desired result

Stochastic parrot: A critical term describing AI language models as systems that mimic human language patterns without truly understanding meaning

Sycophancy: A critical term describing how some chatbots tend to flatter human users and fail to present critical perspectives

Index